PROBLEMS OF THE HEBREW VERBAL SYSTEM

כבוד איש כבוד אביו

PROBLEMS
OF THE
HEBREW VERBAL SYSTEM

BY

G. R. DRIVER, M.A.

FELLOW OF MAGDALEN COLLEGE
AND
READER IN COMPARATIVE SEMITIC PHILOLOGY, OXFORD

OLD TESTAMENT STUDIES

Published under the auspices of the Society for Old Testament Study

NUMBER II.

Edinburgh: T. & T. CLARK, 38 George Street
1936

Râs Šamrah; for I do not think it prudent to use a language which is in course of being deciphered largely with the help of Hebrew to throw light on unsolved problems in Hebrew itself. At the same time I am well aware that they are likely to support what is here said in several respects.

In conclusion, it is my pleasant duty to thank the Society for Old Testament Study for making a generous grant towards the cost of its publication and accepting it as one of the monographs issued under their auspices, and to set on record my appreciation of the fact that the publishers are Messrs. T. & T. Clark, who have often acted in the same capacity for my father.

G. R. DRIVER.

Magdalen College, Oxford.
12th November 1936.

CONTENTS

NOTE

The following instances of the archaic or 'conservative' use of apparent perfect and imperfect tenses from Punic and also from Nabatæan and Samaritan texts are here added to those set out on pp. 116–118 and pp. 120–121 with a view to the completion of the argument.

On pp. 116–118:

Pun. 'there shall belong (*kn*) to the priests the slices (?) and the joints (?)'[1]

'and there shall belong (*wkn*) to the priests the skins of the goats'[2]

Nab. 'And may Dûsharâ curse (*wʿln*) any one who shall bury any one else than him who is written above in this grave'[3]

Sam. 'who will number (*mny*) the dust of Jacob?'[4]

'let there fall (*nplt*) terror upon them'[5]

'how shall I do this great evil and sin (*wḥṭyt*)?'[6]

On pp. 120–121:

Sam. 'the peoples heard (*yšmʿyn*)'[7]

In the Nabatæan passage it is immaterial whether the verb is taken as an example of the optative use of *qátil*[8] with weak *wāw* prefixed to it or whether it is a case of 'consecutive' *wāw* with the perfect tense—in other words, whether *wāw* is essential to the construction, as it seems to be in the second Punic passage.[9] In the Samaritan passages it is important to remark that both such an optative construction and the preterite *yáqtul* may be used even where the Hebrew text employs other constructions, and this fact suggests that these idioms are not, as usually supposed, mere Hebraisms.[10]

All these examples of archaic constructions with the verb then serve to illustrate their wide diffusion and support the view that, wherever they are found, they are common Semitic idioms which have survived with varying degrees of frequency in all the Semitic languages.

1 Cooke, *N.-S.I.* *43.* 8.

2 *Ibid.* *43.* 4; cp. *42.* 4, 6, 8, 10, 11. Elsewhere 'there shall belong (*ykn*) . . .' (*ib.* 3, 13, 15; cp. 7) is used.

3 *Ibid.* *81.* 4–5; cp. *79.* 5. The use of the imperfect tense elsewhere in this phrase, as in 'and let Dûsharâ curse (*wylʿn*) . . .' (*ibid.* *80.* 3, *86.* 8) may be noted by way of contrast.

4 Numb. *23.* 10 (Hebr. *mānāh*).

5 Exod. *15.* 16 (Hebr. *tippōl*).

6 Gen. *39.* 3 (Hebr. *wᵉḥāṭâṯî*).

7 Exod. *15.* 14 (Hebr. *šāmᵉʿû*).

8 Cp. Arab. 'may God curse thee (*laʿanaka*)!' (Wright *Arab. Gramm.* II. 2–3).

9 Cp. Cooke, *op. cit.* *42.* 18, 20.

10 Cp. Uhlemann, *Instit. Ling. Samar.* I. 167–171.

ABBREVIATIONS

'A.A.A.' . . . . . . 'Annals of Archæology and Anthropology' (Liverpool).

'A.B.L.' . . . . . . R. F. Harper, 'Assyrian and Babylonian Letters belonging to the Kouyounjik Collections of the British Museum.'

'A.K.A.' . . . . . . E. A. W. Budge & L. W. King, 'Annals of the Kings of Assyria,' I.

A.Ru. . . . . . . M. David & E. Ebeling, *Assyrische Rechtsurkunden.*[1]

A.S.Kt. . . . . . . P. Haupt, *Akkadische und sumerische Keilschrifttexte.*

A.-T. . . . . J. A. Knudtzon, *Die El-Amarna-Tafeln.*

Ab.B. . . . . A. Ungnad, *Altbabylonische Briefe aus dem Museum zu Philadelphia.*[2]

Abh. z. hebr. Gramm. . . . . F. E. C. Dietrich, *Abhandlungen zur hebräischen Grammatik.*

Act. Orient. . . . . . *Acta Orientalia* (Leyden).

'Amos' . . . . E. A. Edghill, 'The Book of Amos, with Notes, edited . . . by G. A. Cooke.'

Ao.B. . . . . E. Ebeling, B. E. Meissner, E. F. Weidner, *Altorientalische Bibliothek.*

'Arab. Gramm.' . . . . . 'A Grammar of the Arabic Language . . . revised by W. Robertson Smith & M. J. de Goeje' (1933).

Arab. Synt. . . . . . . H. Reckendorf, *Arabische Syntax.*

'Aram. Pap.' . . . . . . A. E. Cowley, 'Aramaic Papyri of the Fifth Century B.C.'

Ass. Gramm. . . . . . . F. Delitzsch, *Assyrische Grammatik* (1906).

'Ass. L.' . . . . . . G. R. Driver & Sir J. C. Miles, 'The Assyrian Laws, edited with Translation and Commentary.'

Assurb. . . . . . . M. Streck, *Assurbanipal und die letzten assyrischen Könige bis zum Untergange Nineveh's.*

B.A.S.S. . . . . . . *Beiträge zur Assyriologie und vergleichenden semitischen Sprachwissenschaft.*

B.B. . . . . A. Ungnad, *Babylonische Briefe aus der Zeit der Hammurapi-Dynastie.*

B.Bussps. . . . . . . H. Zimmern, *Babylonische Busspsalmen.*

'B.H.T.' . . . . . . S. Smith, 'Babylonian Historical Texts relating to the Capture and Downfall of Babylon.'

B.L.B.-D. . . . . . . H. Ranke, 'Babylonian Legal and Business-Documents from the Time of the First Dynasty of Babylon.'

'B.P.P.' . . . . . . S. H. Langdon, 'Babylonian Penitential Psalms.'

B.S.S. . . . . T. Nöldeke, *Beiträge zur semitischen Sprachwissenschaft.*

B.T. . . . . J. N. Strassmaier, *Babylonische Texte . . . von den Thontafeln des Britischen Museums copirt und autographirt.*

Bab.-ass. Gramm. . . . . A. Ungnad, *Babylonisch-assyrische Grammatik mit Übungsbuch (in Transkription)* (1926).

Babyl. . . . . . . *Babyloniaca. Études de philologie assyro-babylonienne.*

---

[1] In the *Zeitschrift der vergleichenden Rechtswissenschaft*, XLIV. 305–381.
[2] *Ibid.* XXXVI. 214–353.

'Behistûn'	L. W. King & R. C. Thompson, 'The Sculptures and Inscription of Darius the Great on the Rock of Behistûn in Persia.'
'C.D.A.L.'	W. Muss-Arnolt, 'A Concise Dictionary of the Assyrian Language.'
'C.I.W.A.'	H. C. Rawlinson, 'Cuneiform Inscriptions of Western Asia.'
'Chronicles'	L. W. King, 'Chronicles concerning Early Babylonian Kings.'
'Coll. Arab.'	G. R. Driver, 'A Grammar of the Colloquial Arabic of Syria and Palestine.'
'Comp. Gramm.' . . .	W. Wright, 'Lectures on the Comparative Grammar of the Semitic Languages.'
'Comp. Gr. of the Sem. Lang.'	De Lacy O'Leary, 'Comparative Grammar of the Semitic Languages.'
'Comp. Syr. Gr.'	T. Nöldeke, 'Compendious Syriac Grammar,' translated from the second and improved German Edition by J. A. Crichton (1904).
'Creation'	S. H. Langdon, 'The Babylonian Epic of Creation.'
'Dict.'	M. Jastrow, 'A Dictionary of the Targumim, the Talmud Babli and Yerushalmi, and the Midrashic Literature.'
'E.N.'	E Chiera, 'Excavations at Nuzi,' I.
'E.N.'	R. H. Pfeiffer, 'Excavations at Nuzi,' II.
E.S.S.	G. Bergsträsser, *Einfuhrung in die semitischen Sprachen. Sprachproben und grammatische Skizzen.*
E.S.St.	H. Torczyner, *Die Entstehung des semitischen Sprachtypus.*
Era	E. Ebeling, *Der akkadische Mythus vom Pestgotte Era.*
Etana	S. H. Langdon, 'The Legend of Etana and the Eagle.'
'Eth. Gramm.'	A. Dillmann, 'Ethiopic Grammar . . . enlarged and improved by C. Bezold, translated by J. A. Crichton' (1907).
Fabel	E. Ebeling, *Die babylonische Fabel und ihre Bedeutung für die Literaturgeschichte.*
G.V.G.S.S.	C. Brockelmann, *Grundriss der vergleichenden Grammatik der semitischen Sprachen.*
'Gilg.'	R. C. Thompson, 'The Epic of Gilgamish.'
'Gr. of the Aram. Id., B.T.' .	C. Levias, 'A Grammar of the Aramaic Idiom contained in the Babylonian Talmud.'
Gramm. d. Bibl.-Aram. . .	E. Kautzsch, *Grammatik des Biblisch-aramäischen.*
Gramm. d. chr.-pal. Aram. .	F. Schultess, *Grammatik des christlich-palästinischen Aramäisch . . . herausgegeben von E. Littmann.*
Gramm. de l'hébr. bibl. . .	P. Joüon, *Grammaire de l'hébreu biblique. Paradigmes et index.*
'H.T.R.'	'Harvard Theological Review' (Cambridge, U.S.A.).
Hamm. Ges.	A. Ungnad, *Hammurabi's Gesetz . . . Syllabische und zusammenhangende Umschrift nebst vollständigem Glossar.*
Hebr. Gramm.	G. Bergsträsser, *Hebräische Grammatik mit Benutzung der von E. Kautzsch bearbeiteten 28. Auflage von Wilhelm Gesenius' hebräischer Grammatik.*

'Hebr. Gramm.' . . .	E. Kautzsch, 'Gesenius' Hebrew Grammar . . . revised in accordance with the 28th German Edition (1909), by A. E. Cowley' (1910).
'Hebr. Lex.' . . .	F. Brown, S. R. Driver, C. A. Briggs, 'A Hebrew and English Lexicon of the Old Testament.'
Hebr. u. Aram. Hwb. . .	F. Buhl, *Hebräisches und aramäisches Handwörterbuch über das Alte Testament* (1921).
Hist. Gr. d. hebr. Spr. . .	H. Bauer & P. Leander, *Historische Grammatik der hebräischen Sprache des Alten Testaments.*
Inschriftenw. Assurb. . .	T. Bauer, *Das Inschriftenwerk Assurbanipals.*
Inscr. sém.	H. Pognon, *Inscriptions sémitiques de la Syrie, de la Mésopotamie et de la région de Mossoul.*
J.As.	*Journal asiatique. Recueil de memoires et de notices relatifs aux études orientales* (Paris).
'J.A.O.S.'	'Journal of the American Oriental Society' (New Haven).
'J.B.L.'	'Journal of Biblical Literature' (Philadelphia).
'J.Q.R.'	'Jewish Quarterly Review' (Philadelphia).
'J.R.A.S.'	'Journal of the Royal Asiatic Society' (London).
'J.T.S.'	'Journal of Theological Studies' (Oxford).
K.A.G.	B. E. Meissner, *Kurzgefasste assyrische Grammatik.*
K.A.T.	E. Schrader, *Die Keilinschriften und das Alte Testament* (1883).
K.B.	E. Schrader, *Keilinschriftliche Bibliothek.*
Lehrb. d. hebr. Spr. . . .	H. Ewald, *Ausführliches Lehrbuch der hebräischen Sprache des alten Bundes* (1870).
Lehrgeb. d. hebr. Spr. . .	F. H. W. Gesenius, *Ausführliches grammatisch-kritisches Lehrgebaüde der hebräischen Sprache mit vergleichung der verwandten Dialekte.*
Lex. Arab.-Lat. . . .	G. W. Freytag, *Lexicon Arabico-Latinum.*
Lex. Syr.	C. Brockelmann, *Lexicon syriacum* (1928).
'L.F.B.D.'	G. R. Driver, 'Letters of the First Babylonian Dynasty.'
M.Ao.G.	*Mitteilungen der altorientalischen Gesellschaft.*
M.F.O.B.	*Mélanges de la faculté orientale, Université Saint-Joseph, Beyrouth* (Beirut).
M.Or.	*Monde Oriental* (Uppsala).
M.U.St.-J.	*Mélanges de l'Université Saint-Joseph, Beyrouth* (Beirut).
'Magic'	L. W. King, 'Babylonian Magic and Sorcery.'
Mand. Gramm.	T. Nöldeke, *Mandäische Grammatik.*
Maql.	K. L. Tallqvist, *Die assyrische Beschwörungsserie* Maqlû.
Mat. z. altakk. Spr. . . .	A. Ungnad, *Materialen zur altakkadischen Sprache (bis zum Ende der Ur-Dynastie).*
'N.-S.I.'	G. A. Cooke, 'A Text-book of North-Semitic Inscriptions.'
N.B.S.S.	T. Nöldeke, *Neue Beiträge zur semitischen Sprachwissenschaft.*
Nb.S.S.	J. Barth, *Die Nominalbildung in den semitischen Sprachen.*
'Nebo'	J. Pinckert, 'Hymnen und Gebete an Nebo.'
Nomina	P. de Lagarde, *Uebersicht über die im Aramäischen, Arabischen und Hebräischen übliche Bildung der Nomina.*

Arabic and possibly also in other Semitic languages, and on the other side to the precative or jussive *yaqtul*, which is found in some form in all these languages. In connection with the use of these forms in Hebrew there arises also the need of discovering why the accentuation of the perfect and imperfect or preterite tenses and the form of the copulative conjunction employed with them in Hebrew varies in accordance with the temporal relation which they bear at the moment of use. A distinct problem arises also out of the different uses to which the terminations *-a* and *-u* respectively are put in those languages which have preserved them.

II

Basis of Semitic Roots

A number of facts suggest that many if not all Semitic roots must have been at some time biconsonantal, even though they are now ostensibly triconsonantal. This thesis is perhaps most easily demonstrated by certain primitive nouns, to which Zimmern [1] has drawn attention.

These, which are here given in their assumed proto-Semitic form, as they are common to most or all of the Semitic languages, fall into four main groups according to the objects which they denote, namely :

(i) human relationships—
ʼb ʻ father ʼ *ʼẖ* ʻ brother ʼ *ʼm* ʻ mother ʼ
bn ʻ son ʼ *ḥm* ʻ father-in-law ʼ *mt* ʻ man, husband ʼ
nš ʻ people ʼ

(ii) parts of the body—
dm ʻ blood ʼ *yd* ʻ hand ʼ *pw* ʻ mouth ʼ *śp* ʻ lip ʼ

(iii) natural objects—
ym ʻ sea ʼ *mw* ʻ water ʼ *ʻṣ* ʻ wood ʼ

(iv) certain common nouns—
ym ʻ day ʼ *šm* ʻ name ʼ *ṯn* ʻ two ʼ

Some of these words retained their primitive biliteral form in one or other of the Semitic languages, others were very soon triliteralized in various ways. Thus, on the one hand, the √*mt* remained to the end purely biliteral, as the Acc. *mutu* and the Eth. *met* ʻ man, husband ʼ show.[2] On the other hand, the √*ym* ʻ day ʼ and the √*ym* ʻ sea ʼ were triliteralized by different means in the various languages, as shown in the following tables :

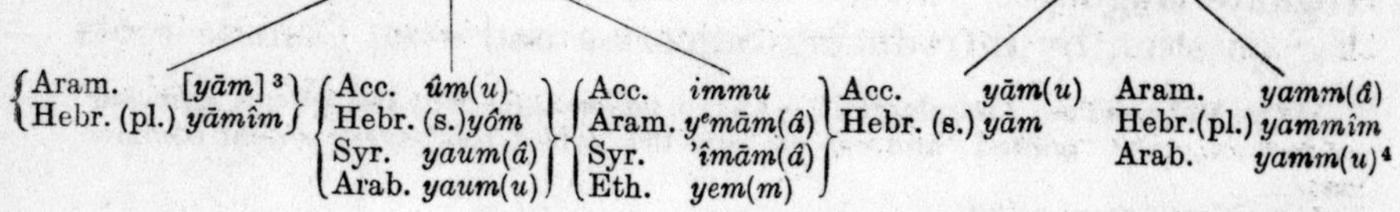
ym ʻdayʼ
ym ʻseaʼ
Aram. [yām] [3]
Hebr. (pl.) yāmîm
Acc. ûm(u)
Hebr. (s.)yôm
Syr. yaum(â)
Arab. yaum(u)
Acc. immu
Aram. yᵉmām(â)
Syr. ʼîmām(â)
Eth. yem(m)
Acc. yām(u)
Hebr. (s.) yām
Aram. yamm(â)
Hebr.(pl.) yammîm
Arab. yamm(u) [4]

[1] In *V.G.S.S.* 163.

[2] Also Hebr. *mᵉṯîm* ʻ men.ʼ

[3] Inferred as the original pronunciation from the two facts that it is written *ym* in early texts and that the *ā* suggests that the Hebr. *yāmîm* is an Aramaizing plural form (s. p. 101).

[4] Possibly an Aramaic loan-word.

These are clear cases of triliteralization; and it is not improbable that, if the $\sqrt{n\check{s}}$ can become the Acc. *nīšu* 'people' and the Aram. *'ĕnāš* 'man,' such words as the Hebr. *'ōzen* 'ear' and *rō'š* 'head' may be also examples of the prolongation by means of ' of primitive biliteral roots. Not a few other roots may be similarly referred to their original forms with more or less probability.

In verbs the same principle of expansion is seen most clearly in the case of onomatopœic roots. Thus it is evident that a common base underlies the Hebr. *'ālāh* 'wailed'=*hālal* 'boasted' (cp. Arab. *halla* 'shouted)=*hêlîl* (cp. Arab. *walwala*) 'howled' or the Hebr. *'ānāh* 'mourned'=*ne'ĕnaḥ* (cp. Aram. *'ănaḥ*) 'groaned'=*hiṯ'ōnēn* (cp. Aram. *'ănan*) 'murmured' =*'ānaq* 'sighed'=*nā'aq* 'groaned'=*nāhag* 'moaned'=*nāhāh* 'lamented'=*nāhaq* 'brayed'; clearly the base is in the first case a shrill liquid cry, in the second a deep nasal sound.[1] Such roots, however, since their formation is common to most if not all languages, are no fair test. It is, therefore, necessary to examine a number of ordinary roots to see whether they exhibit similar principles of development, and examples of various methods adopted to expound various common bases can easily be found.

Thus Wright,[2] who seems to have been one of the first scholars to remark that certain simple bases run through a considerable number of roots common to all the Semitic languages, cites *ḥq* 'slit' and *fl* 'divide' and *qt-qd-qḏ-qṭ* 'cut' in illustration of this point. Hebrew alone affords a good example in *gz-ks-kš-qs/ṣ* 'sever,' which appears in the following words:

gāzaz 'sheared'	*kāsam* 'clipped'	*qāsas* 'sliced off'
gāzal 'stole' [3]	*kāsas* 'cut up'	*qāṣaḇ* 'cut off'
gāzām 'locust' [4]	*kāsap* 'broke' [5]	*qāṣāh* 'cut off'
gāzar 'cut'	*kārap* 'broke off'	*qāšap* 'snapped off'
	kešep 'sorcery' [6]	*qāṣaṣ* 'cut off'

Moreover, numerous variations of this base appear in the cognate languages. So too Ball,[7] who however has complicated the question by introducing Sumerian and even Chinese roots

[1] Cp. Hebr. *nā'am* 'prophesied' (=Arab. *na'ama* groaned) and *nāham* 'growled' =Arab. *naḥama* 'panted' and *naḥara* 'snorted,' which too have a similar common base.

[2] In *Comp. Gramm.* 32.

[3] Arab. *jazala* 'cut off.'

[4] Aram. *gezam* 'cut off.'

[5] Acc. *kasāpu* 'to break (in pieces), to chew' (s. Driver in *Orient.* XII. 63 and *J.T.S.* XXXVI. 404).

[6] Arab. *kasafa* 'cut'; cp. Syr. *'eṯkaššap* 'cut himself (in prayer).'

[7] In *Hilprecht Anniversary Volume*, 41–56.

into the discussion, examines several such bases; of these the most widely spread is *dr-ṭr-tr* and *zr-sr-ṣr-śr-šr* ' surround ' or ' turn round,' which he finds underlying the following verbs and nouns (to which a few others are here added):

Acc.	*dūru* ' enclosing wall '	Arab.	*târa* ' hovered round '	Acc.	*târu* ' to return '
Hebr.	*dôr* ' circuit (of time) '		*ṭawr(u)* ' border '	Hebr.	*tûr* ' to go round '
Arab.	*dawr(u)* ' period '	Hebr.	*ṭîrāh* ' encampment '		*tôr* ' plait '
	dâr(u) ' dwelling '		*'āṭar* ' shut up '		*kittēr* ' surrounded '
Hebr.	*ḥeḏer* ' enclosed chamber '	Arab.	*'aṭara* ' bent round '		
Syr.	*ḥdar* ' went round '	Hebr.	*'āṭar* ' surrounded '		
		Syr.	*qṭar* ' bound '		

Aram.	*zîr* ' to compress '	Acc.	*sîru* ' ring-wall '
Syr.	*zwar* ' compressed '	Hebr.	*sûr* ' to turn aside '
Hebr.	*zēr* ' circlet '		*sārar* ' was rebellious ' [1]
Arab.	*zarra* ' drew together '		*sōhar* ' prison '
Aram.	*ḥăzar* ' encircled '	Acc.	*saḫāru* ' to go round '
Hebr.	*'āzar* ' girded '	Hebr.	*'āsar* ' bound '
		Aram.	*s^erag̱* ' entwined '
		Hebr.	*śārag̱* ' intertwined '
Hebr.	*ṣûr* ' to besiege '	Hebr.	*šûr* ' wall '
	ṣārar ' tied up '		*šōr* ' navel-cord '
	'aṣara ' stored up '		*šērāh* ' bracelet ' [2]
Arab.	*'aṣara* ' confined '	Aram.	*š^erar* ' was hard ' [3]
	ḥaṣara ' surrounded '	Hebr.	*šārîḏ* ' muscle ' [4]
Hebr.	*ḥāṣēr* ' enclosure '		*šarš^erāh* ' chain '
	'āṣar ' restrained '		*qāšar* ' bound '
	'ăṣereṯ ' band (of people) '		
Acc.	*qaṣāru* ' to bind '		

Such tables irresistibly suggest that the Semitic vocabulary probably originated with a limited number of biconsonantal bases, and that the bulk of these were converted already in the prehistoric period into triconsonantal roots either by repeating the second consonant or by the addition of various formative elements.

The process of expansion, however, can be seen almost at work within the historic period; for such an assumption will alone account for the large number of apparently shortened forms or alternative types of weak verbs which are still current in classical Hebrew. These, too, beyond any doubt indicate the artificial triliteralization of primitive biliteral roots. Examples of biconsonantal, though often ostensibly triconsonantal, forms may be seen in *raḇ* ' was great ' from the √*rbb* and *rāḇ* ' contended ' from the √*ryb* and in *wayyiḇn* ' and he built ' from the √*bny* and *wayyāḇen* ' and he understood ' from the √*byn*. Far commoner, however, are the instances of alternative forms of the same root obviously going

[1] As turning away from one's duty.
[2] Acc. *šemiru* and *šewiru* ' bracelet.'
[3] As well-knit.
[4] As binding the limbs together.

back to the same base; indeed, a study of the dictionaries of the various Semitic languages will furnish numerous examples of this process of expansion, of which a few typical examples are given in the accompanying table.[1]

If, then, the formative or expanding elements are as varied as they seem from the present discussion to be, caution ought to be exercised before attempting to force all the roots derived from a common base into a single mould; for example, if *gl* may be expanded into *gālal* and *gā'al* and *gā'al* 'soiled,' the expansion of *šh* into *šā'āh*[2] as well as into *šā'āh* and of *tb* into *tā'ēḇ*[3] as well as into *tā'ēḇ* 'loathed' is equally legitimate, and emendation becomes unjustifiable in either case. The variations reflect partly the different sources from which Hebrew is derived and partly the dialects into which it must to some extent have been broken up and of which the Massoretes have unfortunately destroyed almost all traces.[4]

Other rare forms of expansion also occur: for example, Burney[5] cites that of a √*šl* into *šûl* and *šōḇel* 'skirt' and of a √*śk*, whence *śûḵ* and *śāḵaḵ* 'intertwine' are derived, into *śᵉḇāḵāh* 'net-work' and *śᵉmîḵāh* 'blanket'; but these are really only variations of the same process due to the interchange of *b-w-m*, which is of frequent occurrence in the Semitic languages.

This principle of expansion is, however, extended yet further. In the first place, the formation of many nominal types is based on it, and the derived stems or themes of the regular verb owe their development to it. In the second place, the same process continues operative in the extension of triliteral into quadriliteral and even quinqueliteral roots in various ways. Thus, although the causative *ša*-theme properly died out with Accadian, Syriac uses not only *mallî* but also *šamlî* 'filled,' and modern Arabic uses both *qalaba* and also colloquially *saqlaba* 'upset.' Again, medial expansion occurs already in Hebrew and Aramaic, and may be illustrated by the Hebr. *za'ap=zil'āpah* 'raging' and by the Hebr. *sᵉ'appāh =sar'appāh* 'bough' and the Syr. *sûr'âpâ* 'branching (of boughs)'; so too modern Arabic has lengthened *barrad* into *baurad* 'cooled' and *farraš* into *faršā* 'spread,' thus turning the derived theme of a triliteral into a brand-new quadriliteral verb. Finally, the commonest method of expansion seems to have been by the reduplication of the last or last two consonants, whereby triliteral are converted into quadri-

[1] S. p. 7. The 3rd person of the Qa lis not always in use but is inferred from other extant forms.
[2] Gen. *24*. 21. [3] Am. *6*. 8. [4] S. pp. 98–107.
[5] In *Judges*, 92; cp. xiii, xvi, 40, 69. [6] Driver, *Coll. Arab.* 77–78.

Base.	Expansion. Initial.	Medial.	Final.	Meaning.
' b	... ... yā'aḇ ... tā'aḇ [1]	... 'āhaḇ [2]	... 'āḇāh	'incline'
b l	'āḇal ... ... nāḇal ...	... ...	... bālāh	'wear out'
g l	... ...	gā'al ... ... gāʿal	gālal	'defile'
h m	... ...	... ... hûm	hāmam hāmāh	'be noisy'
ḥ m	... ... yāḥam	... ...	ḥāmam (ḥmâ)	'be hot'
ṭ b	... ... yāṭaḇ	(ṭᵉ'ēḇ) ... ṭûḇ	... ...	'be good'
k l	... ... yāḵōl	... (kᵉhēl)[2] kûl	... ...	'comprehend'
l k	... hālaḵ [yālaḵ]	... ...	... ...	'go'
m s	... ...	mā'as	māsas māsāh	'melt'
m š	... ... yāmaš	... ...	māšaš ... māšaḥ ...	'touch'
p ḥ	... ... yāpaḥ nāpaḥ ...	... ... pûᵃḥ	... ...	'puff'
p r	... ...	... ...	... pārāh pāraḥ (praʿ)	'sprout'
ṣ ḥ	... ... nāṣaḥ ...	... ...	ṣāḥaḥ ṣāḥāh	'be bright'
r b	... ... yārēḇ [3]	... ...	rāḇaḇ rāḇāh	'be great'
r n	... ...	... ... rûn	rānan rānāh	'ring out'
r š	... ... yāraš	rā'ăs ... rûš rîš ...	... ...	'be poor'
š g	... ...	... ... šûg	šāgag šāgāh ... šāgaʿ	'go wrong'
š m	'āšam ... yāšam	... ...	šāmēm	'be appalled'
š p	... ...	šā'ap ... šûp	šāpap šāpāh	'crush'

[1] Cp. Acc. (*w*)*abālu*=*tabālu* 'to carry off' and *idū*=*tidū* 'to know.'

[2] Cp. Hebr. *bôš*=Aram. *bᵉhēṯ* 'was ashamed' and Hebr. *rûṣ*=Aram. *rᵉhēṭ* 'ran.' Albright (in *J.B.L.* XLVI. 177–178) suggests that *'Aḇrām* thus became *'Aḇrāhām* (cp. $\sqrt{r'm}$=*rwm*=*rmm* 'be high') by infixing *h* after the Aramaic fashion, as in these two verbs; but this view is open to the two objections that *rām* for *rôm* (s. p. 100) is itself the Aramaic form of this root (s. Bauer, *Sprachmischung*, 21–26), and that it is difficult to see how the patriarch's name can have been Aramaized not while he was resident in or was passing through Syrian territory, but when he had reached southern Palestine, where Aramaic influence was unlikely. I therefore still prefer the view which I (in *J.B.L.* XLV. 324–325) following Cowley have expressed that the *h* is (not so much a *litera prolongationis* as) a *mater lectionis* (cp. Moab. *Mhdb'*=Hebr. *Mêdᵉḇā'*=Arab. *Mâdibâ*); for it is not necessary to assume with Albright that the change originally took place in the living or spoken language, and it may rather be suggested that the story explaining its meaning was invented to account for a form found in some written genealogy. Thus too *h* is found written as an obvious *mater lectionis* in the Minæan inscriptions (as in *mhn*=*mn* 'who?' and in *bhns*=*bnsw* 'his sons'), where it is obviously a mere matter of orthography and cannot represent either divergent pronunciations or Aramaizing forms (cp. Weber, *St.aa. Ak.* III. 54, and Rhodokanakis, *St. L. G. Asa.* I. 12–56); and it is noticeable that this *h* occurs almost exclusively in words containing only two radical letters (cp. Hommel, *Süd-ar. Chrest.* 7–8).

[3] G. R. Driver in *J.T.S.* XXXVI. 295.

literal or even quinqueliteral roots; thus the Syr. *ša'en* 'pacified' shows the original root from which the Hebr. *ša'ănan* 'was at ease' has been formed, and *sāḥar* 'went round' is equally clearly the source of *s^eḥarḥar* 'palpitated.'[1] This last class has increased with time and, while fairly common in Arabic, is extremely numerous in Ethiopic.

It seems then that the expansion of shorter into longer roots, which is here postulated as a factor in the development of the ancient Semitic languages, lingers on still as an influence in the formation of the modern dialects. At bottom it is probably analogous to the process whereby many other languages strengthen roots of which the force is continually being weakened in daily use by the addition of prepositional and other elements which give them precision as well as weight.

[1] S. pp. 5–6 for *s r* as the base of *sāḥar* and therefore also of *s^eḥarḥar*.

III

Formation of States and Tenses

Bauer[1] holds that the original verbal form or tense was *yaqtul*, which he calls the 'short aorist,' for the three reasons that the imperative which usually preserves the primitive form of the verb in its purest form shows the closest resemblance to it, that the rich variety of the forms of the aorist and imperative, in which triliteralization is not yet complete, as compared with the uniformity of the other tenses argues its primitive nature, since uniformity is a late development in speech, and that the prefixes of *yaqtul*, which obviously represent personal pronouns, reflect an older period of the language than the affixes of the nominal *qatil*. Thus, for example, in the former there is as yet no distinction in the second person between gender and number, since the prefix *ta-* is used for masculine or feminine, singular or plural subjects indiscriminately, whereas in the latter they are distinguished as *-ta* or *-ti* and *-tumu* or *-tinna* respectively.

The close connection between aorist, imperative, and infinitive, suggests that originally the same form, roughly as in English, served alike as infinitive, imperative, and finite verb: for example, *qum* 'to arise,' *qum* 'arise (thou)' and *ta-qum* 'thou (dost) arise.' This relationship, however, should not be misunderstood, as though the finite verb had been developed out of the infinitive or imperative just as little as the English 'I arise' should be regarded as a combination of the pronoun with the infinitive or imperative. In other words, as the English 'arise' is at one and the same time an imperative or infinitive or finite verb and no priority can be assigned to one or the other of these uses, so it must be assumed that a proto-Semitic *qutul* was used at one and the same time as an imperative or an infinitive and could also be conjugated as a finite verb by the simple device of prefixing a pronominal element to it, whereby *ya-qutul* 'he does kill' and other persons were formed; and this development of the imperfect out of a form common to it and the imperative and infinite is another argument in favour of its priority to the permansive or perfect forms.

[1] In *B.A.S.S.* VIII. i. 5–19; cp. Bauer & Leander, *Hist. Gr. d. hebr. Spr.* I. 268–272.

So long as the aorist was the only form capable of expressing the pronominal subject, it could naturally express no definite time. It was neither subjective, expressing a past or present or future state or action, nor objective, describing a state or act as complete or incomplete, nascent or emergent or the reverse; it was, indeed, like the Chinese and probably like the Indo-Germanic verb, timeless or rather universal, and the actual time was determined partly from the context, partly by the use of adverbs which defined it. We must feel the connection of our verb with the time of the action as a restriction on the expression of our thoughts; consequently, when we use the present in gnomic or universal statements, as in 'cats catch rats,' there is an incongruence between speech and thought, since we are using a form expressive of the time of the act to describe a timeless or universal act. We must, however, conceive the proto-Semitic language as possessing a universal verb of the form *yaqtul*, in which men could in the most primitive times express verbal relations; and this form not only could naturally express what was itself timeless but also could be used for the relation of historical facts, inasmuch as the time of the act might either be inferred from the situation or be indicated by the use of helping words.

If then *yaqtul* was the original verbal form, how did *yaqtulu* arise? For, this being so, it cannot henceforth be regarded as the original form out of which the shorter arose by apocopation. Now in the Accadian language *yaqtulu* is confined to relative clauses, at least in the earlier documents, although it is more widely used or perhaps misused in later texts. Therefore it may be inferred that it originated in relative clauses; and, if this is so, it may be conjectured that it arose out of the resumptive pronoun referring back to the antecedent, as seen in the Acc. *ḫīṭ aḫṭū* (<*aḫṭahu*) 'the sin (which) I sinned (it),'[1] and that from this simple type of relative clause it spread into other dependent clauses and finally made its way into main clauses, thus giving rise to *yaqtulu* as a form of the finite verb. In Arabic, in which alone this longer form of the finite verb appears, the shorter *yaqtul* was confined to the jussive and to close dependence on certain particles where a resumptive pronoun is unthinkable. It is therefore wrong to see a jussive in every *yaqtul*; its jussive use is only an offshoot of its old universal function.

The later tense-form *qata/i/ula* arose out of the affixing of the pronominal elements to the nominal forms *qata/i/ul*. The schematic uniformity of these forms, whereby almost all active verbs are *qatal* and those descriptive of a permanent

[1] Rawlinson, *C.I.W.A.* IV. 10 a. 45 (s. p. 16).

state *qatul*, points unmistakably to the fact that they are modelled on a type already in existence and are therefore secondary formations; further, the pronouns attached to them, inasmuch as the forms of the second person vary according to the gender and number, are later than those with the aorist. Therefore *qata/i/ula* is younger than *yaqtu/a/il*. This process repeated itself subsequently in the individual languages, namely in the Accadian permansive as seen in *šarrāku* 'I am king' and *ṣabtāku* 'I am an acquirer'='I have acquired,' and the Syriac participial formation as seen in *qāṭel-(')nâ* 'I am a killer'='I kill.' So soon, however, as this principle had grown up and the verbal form *qatal-nā* 'we are killers' had established itself beside *naqtul* 'we kill,' verbs of the form *qatal* began to be coined directly from the aorist *yaqtul* without any intermediary *nomen agentis*, whatever the vocalization of the latter might be; and indeed *qatil* and *qatul* (occurring also as *qatīl* and *qa tūl*) represent adjectives, while on the contrary *qatal* (probably originally *qatāl*) represents a *nomen agentis* which could have been formed from every verb and whose form this too might also have. Only those verbs which already from the beginning exhibited the form *qatal* (as *ya-šamaʿ* and *ya-balaʿ*) chose as *nomen agentis* the form *qatil* (as *šamiʿ* and *baliʿ*); and consequently in the case of *qatila* a twofold source, according as it is primary or secondary, must be sought. The following examples exhibit this development: of the primitive *qatil-* form and *qatul*-form, *kabid-tā* 'thou art heavy' and *qatun-tā* 'thou art small'; of the *qatāl*>*qatal-* form, *qatāl-tā* 'thou art a killer'>*qatal-tā* 'thou hast killed'; of the secondary *qatil*-form, *šamiʿ-tā* 'thou art hearing.'[1]

If, then, it is granted that such imperfects as *ya-šamaʿ* and *ya-balaʿ* rested upon an adjectival form *qatil* like the participle *qātil* in the later development of the Semitic languages, *i.e.* as a secondary formation, and so subsequently formed *šamiʿ* and *baliʿ* as their perfects, two difficulties disappear. First, it is no longer necessary to assume a most improbable neuter sense on the supposition that, being of the form *qatil*, they were neuter or intransitive, *e.g.* to suppose that *šamiʿ* and *baliʿ* originally denoted the state of hearing and swallowing respectively in a purely neuter sense; and, second, it becomes intelligible why the imperfect *yaqtal* corresponded with the perfect *qatila*. Further, verbs of the form *qatal*, in which *yaqtul* is secondary, will have appeared very soon, even if it is not always as easy to prove as, for example, in the case of the Pers. *rizq* 'sustenance,' from which the

[1] S. pp. 47–48.

Arab. *razaqa* 'sustained' has been coined, where the imperfect *yarzuqu* is demonstrably not the original form from which the perfect is derived.

Like *qatala*, so also did *qatila* and *qatula* arise. In the first instance primitive adjectives like *šalim* 'well' and *qatun* 'small' gave rise in combination with pronominal elements to the verbal forms *šalim-tā* 'thou art well' and *qatun-tā* 'thou art small.' So soon as this pattern was developed, adjectives of other forms assimilated themselves to these when combined with pronominal elements to form verbs, as the Arab. *ṣali/uba* 'was hard' was formed from *ṣulb* 'hard.' In fact, many types of Semitic adjectives are no more derived from verbs than is the Lat. *aeger* derived from *aegrotare*; they are rather descended from proto-Semitic adjectives, although this does not exclude the possibility that there are also many secondary adjectives derived from verbs.

The distinction between *qatil* and *qatul* was not original but grew up like that between *-like* and *-ish*, as seen in 'child-like' and 'child-ish,' in English, the form 'child-ish' being due to the analogy of 'thiev-ish.' So *qatil* attached itself to transitory characteristics on the analogy of the primitive *zaqin* 'old' and *qatul* to permanent characteristics on the analogy of the primitive *qatun*. This same principle explains the distinction between *qatila* (*yaqtal*) and *qatala* (*yaqtul* or *yaqtil*). The usual theory that *qatala* denotes action and *qatila* transitory conditions is far from exact, as many examples show: thus the Hebr. *'ābad* 'perished'[1] is intransitive and the Arab. *baliʿa* 'swallowed' is really transitive, while the Acc. *itbal* 'carried off' is also transitive,[2] each the reverse of what would be expected from its forms. The distinction indeed between these forms is not logical but historical and can be found only by inquiring to which class each verb belongs. Then, as the nominals *qatal-tā* and *šamiʿ-tā* acquired the aorists *ta-qtul* and *ta-šmaʿ* respectively, so in the same way to the nominals *kabid-tā* and *qatun-tā* there were formed the aorists *ta-kbad* and *ta-qtun* respectively; but the form *ta-qtun* occurred less frequently and was often replaced by *ta-qtan*. It is easy, too, to see how, as the original imperfect *tašmaʿ* acquired a perfect *šamiʿ*, so perfects derived from adjectives like *šalim* had imperfects of the form *yašlam*, and how on the

[1] Yet Acc. *abit* beside Pal. *abadat* (Knudtzon, *A.-T. 288*, 52) ought to be a warning against laying too much stress on the vocalization of the derived languages as representing a primitive or proto-Semitic pronunciation; for the assimilation plays a considerable and often unsuspected part in vocalization (s. p. 47).

[2] Haupt (in *J.A.O.S.* XVI. ci.–cii.) attempts to distinguish *qatala* as expressing voluntary and *qatila* as expressing involuntary action; but this suggestion fails to explain many even of his own examples.

analogy of the imperative *šamaʿ* from *šamiʿ-tā* there arose in the case of *śabiʿ-ṯā* 'thou art satisfied' an imperative *śabaʿ* 'be satisfied.'

The development of the later *qatala*, as distinct from the earlier *qatila* and *qatula*, marks the end of timelessness; for it encroached on the sphere previously occupied by *yaqtul* and so drove that into a region as yet unoccupied. Only at this stage of development is it proper to speak of tenses in the Semitic languages. Now the originally nominal *qatala* could describe two kinds of action, namely, 'he is conqueror' = 'he has conquered,' which is an action once for all completed and so belonging to the completed past, and 'he is a striver' = 'he strives,' which is a lasting or repeated action embracing an element of the past but completing itself in the present or future. Some words tend to vary with the context: *e.g.* a 'writer' is either a person 'who has written' a letter (Gk. γράψας) or a professional 'scribe' (Gk. γραμματεύς); but it is unlikely that such opposed uses would be long retained side by side in the same verbal form. An adjustment to one side or the other would probably occur: either the present or the perfect meaning would predominate. In practice in the West-Semitic languages *qatal* took on the perfect, in the East-Semitic languages *ya-qatal* took on the present significance; consequently *yaqtul* became in the former a present and in the latter a preterite tense. The development of the Semitic tenses, however, did not proceed so simply as this. Thus the Hebrew *qāṭal* continued to be widely used as a present (namely with consecutive *wāw*), and in the South-Semitic languages the Arab. *qátala* and more rarely the Eth. *qatála* still exhibit traces of such a usage; yet the Acc. *iqaṭal* (that is, *i-qaṭal* corresponding with the proto-Semitic *qatal*) [1] shows no trace of any earlier use as a perfect tense. These facts, then, show that the present significance of *qatala* must have prevailed in the common speech of the primitive Semites over the whole territory, and that it must therefore have had this force originally in the Western languages.

Thus *qatala* appears in the first place as a conjugated verbal noun, in the next in the time-sphere of a present participle. But, as such a participle is not solely present but expresses also the imperfect (as in the Lat. *sede vacante* 'while the see is' or 'was vacant') and the future (as in the Engl. 'it is being done to-morrow') according to the context, so also *qatala* served these three functions. In the Semitic sphere the Syr. *qāṭel-(')nā* 'I am killing' shows the transition of a participle

[1] Christian (in *Anthropos* XIV.–XV. 733), objects that this equation leaves the Eth. *yeqatel* beside *yeqtel* unexplained (s. pp. 63, 93–94).

into a genuine tense, and it may therefore be assumed that *qatala* went through the same process of development. Now this Syriac participle designated momentary and also lasting acts or states in the present and thus entirely ousted the imperfect; further, it often served as a future, whether the circumstance was brought vividly before the mind's eye as present or the context was sufficient to refer the otherwise undefined representation of it to the future; and, finally, in circumstantial clauses it described contemporaneous occurrences in past time. Such too must have been the functions of *qatala* in the primitive Semitic speech; for all the later uses of it in the various languages can be brought under these heads. In many cases, moreover, it remained open to the individual language to employ either the older *yaqtul* or the younger *qatala*; in certain idioms, however, the use of the new form was probably firmly established at a quite early period, while *yaqtul* after as before remained the tense proper to narration.

At this point, while the development of the verbal system was in full stream, when the relationship of *yaqtul* to *qatala* was still fluctuating and imperfectly defined, Accadian turned aside from the common speech of the Semitic family and went its own way, though without diverging very far from it. In the West-Semitic languages *qatala* was further developed, whereby the whole relation of the tense was completely inverted. Here the perfect significance underlying the conception of 'killer' as 'one who has killed' in the nominal *qatal* took full effect and was carried over into the whole stock of verbs, and thereby the form was appropriated to serve as the tense of narration, like the European perfect. Consequently *yaqtul* lost its narrative function and was restricted to its former ill-defined uses, which may be described as approximating to those of a present participle. Thus the two verbal forms almost exchanged their respective functions as compared with those exercised by them in the original Semitic speech. But this interchange was not uniformly carried out: each form retained sporadic traces of its primitive functions, and above all there survived from them certain more or less stereotyped idioms of frequent occurrence which did not take part in the new developments. Especially where the verbal form was closely connected with a particle in any special usage the spirit of conservatism showed itself stronger than the impulse to change; consequently such collocations, for example, as the Hebr. *'āz* with the imperfect as applied to the description of an event in past time were not upset by the revolution taking place in the language but remained in use unchanged. In no Semitic language is the incongruity between form and function entirely eliminated.

It may at once be admitted that Bauer has made several good points in the course of his discussion. Such is the observation that the same form in all probability served several different purposes (as also it may do in other languages: *e.g.* the English 'were' may be either a plural indicative or a singular or plural subjunctive form). Further, he is clearly right in maintaining that the Hebrew construction with consecutive *wāw* is inexplicable on the theory that the perfect expressed complete and the imperfect tense incomplete action, and that the cohortative was at any rate primarily unconnected with the jussive forms, inasmuch as these were applicable also to past time. Lastly, his suggestion that many verbs, like the Arabic *ṣali/uba*, though of a primitive form, are in fact secondary formations, may be accepted without hesitation. Yet the theory which he propounds cannot be regarded as satisfactory, and many objections can be brought against it both generally and in detail; some of these objections hardly require explanation or amplification, while the reasons for them and the force of others will come to light in the course of subsequent enquiry.

At the outset, Bergsträsser[1] raises the general and indeed weighty objection to Bauer's theory that the co-existence of two layers of usage belonging to two different periods and based on principles exactly the opposite of one another is in the highest degree improbable, especially when it is not safeguarded by special conditions such as poetical idiom or archaic and stereotyped (*e.g.* legal) phraseology, and he goes on to object that it fails to satisfy all the conditions of the Semitic and especially of the Hebrew tenses, as indeed a glance at any table of their various usages at once suggests; moreover, he shows that it leaves the origin of the active *qatal* essentially unexplained, since the *nomen agentis* of the form *qatāl* which is postulated to account for it is purely hypothetical, while König[2] adds that not this but *qâtil* is its true and normal type. Other difficulties will become apparent during the progress of the present examination, but three may be stated here as they will hardly come into the following discussion. First, Bauer's argument that the varieties of the aorist and imperative forms are evidence of the priority of *yaqtul* and *qutul* as against *qatil* may be two-edged; for it may be argued with equal justification that every form, however manifold are the varieties of it even in the earliest period of a language, must at

[1] In *Hebr. Gramm.* II. 9; cp. *O. Lz.* XXVI. 257–260, 477.
[2] In *Z.D.M.G.* LXV. 719–720.

some time have been derived from a single simple form. For example, Accadian has only one form, Hebrew and Aramaic and Ethiopic have several, and Arabic has a multiplicity of infinitive forms ; here, then, there is a progressive increase in the number of forms as time goes on. Moreover, as König[1] shows, the permansive *qati/u/al* exhibits at bottom as many varieties of vocalization as the imperfect *yaqtu/i/al*, so that the argument is in any case not decisive. Second, if the active *qatal* has arisen out of a *nomen agentis* of the form *qatāl* (on the supposition that there is or has been such a form), it is easy to account for the accentuation of the masculine *qāṭál*, while the feminine *qā́ṭᵉlāh* may be explained as due to a desire to differentiate it from the adjectival feminine singular form ; but this hypothesis makes the accentuation of the singular and plural forms of the first and the singular form of the second person with consecutive *wāw* quite inexplicable.[2] At the same time Bauer appears to leave also the peculiar accentuation of the Hebrew imperfect tense with consecutive *wāw* without explanation.[3] Third, he leaves the *-a* of *qatala* entirely without comment or explanation and puts forward a solution of the subjunctive *-u* as seen in the Accadian *iqṭulu* which cannot for a moment be accepted. For against his suggestion that it arose out of the pronominal suffix *-ahu* 'him,' which was used in relative clauses to refer back to the antecedent, it can be argued that, if this were the origin of the ending *-u*, this vowel would be long (like the Hebrew *-ahu*>*-ōh*>*-ô*), since it would be the result of contraction, whereas in fact it is short, and that it is odd that it has survived only in that language which had the totally different *-šu* and has disappeared in those which had the required *-ahu*>*ōh*>*ô* as the pronominal suffix of the third person.

Bergsträsser[4] thinks that *qutul* and *yaqtul*, which is in its short form devoid of any afformative addition and terminates in a consonant, are the original verbal forms : starting from *qutul*, the short *yaqtul* first acquired a jussive sense ; then there fell to it as the sole verbal form for expressing assertion the duty of expressing also the past, since the nominal form was at hand to express the present. This double duty which fell to *yaqtul* is preserved in the Accadian preterite *iqṭul* and precative *liqṭul*, in the Hebrew jussive *yiqṭōl* and the preterite *way-yiqṭōl*, and partially in the Arabic jussive *yaqtul* and negative *yaqtul* with *lam(mâ)* 'not (yet)' and certain other particles. The antiquity of *yaqtul* is attested by the

[1] In *Z.D.M.G.* LXV. 718–719.
[2] S. pp. 88, 89–90.
[3] S. pp. 88, 90–91.
[4] In *Hebr. Gramm.* II. 9–14 (s. Hempel in *Z.At.W.* XLV. 236–237).

wide diffusion of this form in the Hamitic languages. Its vocalization varied much, so long as it was not biradical, *i.e.* having only one vowel; but it soon became uniform through the influence of various factors.

Equally early and side by side with this form was developed the possibility of affixing pronominal afformatives to nouns, as seen in the Accadian *šarrāku*, formed out of *šarr*^{um} + *(an)āku*, 'I (am) king.' In this way there grew up an afformative conjugation, as distinct from the preformative *yaqtul*, formed originally out of the adjectival *qatil* and *qatul*;[1] and from this twofold vocalization it may be inferred that the permansive and perfect, in spite of the antiquity of the afformative conjugation, only arose as a verbal form when the vocalization was already in process of becoming effective as a formative element. Almost all Accadian permansives and many Western perfects are of the form *qatil* or *qatul*. Beside *qatil* and *qatul* there was also a neutral perfect *qatal* at hand but, owing to its infrequent use, it had little influence on the subsequent development of this tense.[2] As afformatives only gender and number were marked in the third person, the former in the feminine form by *-at* and the latter in the plural form by *-u*; in the second and third persons the person was marked by pronominal elements with the deictic *an-*, the second person by *-tā* (<-[*an*]-*tā*), *-tī*, *-tumū*, *-tinnā*, and the first person by *-āku* and *-nā* (<-[*an*]-*nā*). The meaning of this afformative conjugation was very close to a general or universal present. Its antiquity is further confirmed, apart from the unanimity of all the Semitic languages in exhibiting it in their earliest known forms, by the fact that it occurs with the same meaning in the Egyptian and Berber as in the Semitic languages.

From the jussive-preterite *yaqtul* there split off a present-future tense, though in different ways in the East and the West. In the East an accented *-a-* was inserted between the first and second radicals, as in the Acc. *iqáṭal* from *iqṭul*; in the West various vowels were added at the end of the word, as in the Arab. *yaqtulu* or *yaqtula* from *yaqtul*. Since however in Accadian *-u* is added to all tenses in subordinate clauses,[3] it is possible that this present-future had already split off from the jussive-preterite in the primitive Semitic speech, and only the infixing of *-a-*, as in the Acc. *iqáṭal*, and the differentiation of the forms with *-u* and *-a*, as in the Arab. *yaqtulu* and *yaqtula*, are late. The view that the infixed *-a-* and the

[1] Or, for example, *mit* and *buš* in the case of originally biliteral roots.

[2] Lagarde (*Nomina*, 25–52) and Hommel (in *Z.D.M.G.* XLIV. 536–537) and Zimmern (in *Z.A.* V. 11), also think that *qatil* and *qatul* are older than *qatal* (s. pp. 25–26).

[3] Sarauw (in *Festschrift Thomsen* 67–68) connects this Acc. *-u* with the Arab. *-u* (s. pp. 75–77).

affixed -*u* are early is supported by the fact that affixed and infixed vowels are frequently used in the Hamitic languages as tense-signs, and also by the fact that the usages of the Accadian present and the West-Semitic imperfect tenses show mutual connections.

While Accadian remained essentially stationary at this stage of development, the Western languages further developed their system. The form *qatal* from signifying a universal present went on to acquire the force of an Indo-Germanic perfect, *i.e.* the power to describe a present state arising out of a past event, and also the force of a German perfect, *i.e.* the power to express the statement of past events without reference to the events preceding them: for example, *mit*= 'he has died' and 'he is dead' (Gk. τέθνηκε), and *zaqin*= 'he has grown old' and 'he is old' (Gk. γεγήρακε). To the past tense which had thus arisen there was then added an imperfect on the analogy of the old present-imperfect *yaqtul*, and subsequently a jussive-preterite was newly formed: for example, *yamut* 'he dies' and *yamut* 'he died' (Gk. ἀπέθανε) and also 'may he die.'[1]

In the choice of vowels in the imperfect, so far as analogy did not prevail, as in *yamut* from *maut*, the principle of polarity operated. The full vowel *a* in the imperfect took the place of the reduced vowel *i*/*u* in the perfect, which incidentally shows that the Arab. *qatula-yaqtulu* with the same vowels in both tenses is a secondary scheme; and possibly, too, the vowels in *qatil-yiqtal* and *qatul-yuqtal*[2] are due to the same principle.[3] As the neutral scheme *qati*/*ul* was to *yiqtal*, so to the old imperfect (preterite-jussive and present) *yaqti*/*ul* an active perfect *qatal* was newly formed; and the choice of *a* as its vowel was due partly to the same principle of polarity, whereby perfect and imperfect took the opposite vowels, partly to the fact that opposition to the old neutral *qati*/*ul* demanded *a* in the new form. The old active *a*-imperfects followed in a lesser degree the neutral scheme (*i.e.* the new formation of an *i*-perfect), in a greater degree they passed over into *i*/*u*-imperfects in consequence of the now prevalent predominance of the neutral significance in the *a*-imperfect.

The perfect then did not remain restricted to the statement of past events but was developed, as it often was in the Indo-Germanic languages, into a narrative tense and so began to encroach on the old preterite; but the distribution of functions

[1] Cp. Knudtzon in *Z.A.* VII. 34–37, 55–57; Joüon in *M.F.O.B.* V. i. 359–360.

[2] Ungnad (in *B.A.S.S.* V. 241–243) cites *yāk̲ōl-yûk̲al* 'he is able' as the only surviving example of this scheme.

[3] Ungnad (in *Z.D.M.G.* LIX. 766–768) is in favour of and Brockelmann (*G.V.G.S.S.* I. 601) is against this explanation.

between the two tenses had different results in the individual Western languages. In Aramaic and Ethiopic the preterite entirely disappeared, while Arabic retained it after *lam* and *lammâ* and other particles, wherein polarity again came in, just as in the Hamitic speeches it led to the use of the opposite tenses in negative to those used in affirmative statements.[1] In Hebrew the old preterite is found almost exclusively with consecutive *wāw*, apart from poetry. Here the original distinction of meaning between the perfect and the preterite is reflected, inasmuch as the former stated a fundamental fact, the latter described its further continuation; apart from this, polarity played its part not only in the antithesis entailed in the construction whereby the perfect was followed by consecutive *wāw* with the imperfect, approximately in the same way as the narrative perfect is followed by the imperfect in Berber,[2] but also originally probably in the other negative perfect (which is always employed in existent Hebrew) in relation to the affirmative consecutive imperfect which is at least predominant in existent Hebrew. Finally to this contrasted pair, namely the perfect followed by consecutive *wāw* with the imperfect, is to be added another contrasted pair, namely the imperfect followed by the consecutive perfect, wherein the polar scheme attained its completion. This development is illustrated by the universally present significance, which is now lost, of the old neutral perfects.

Bergsträsser is without doubt right in supposing that *qatil* and *qatul* are older than *qatal*, and additional reasons in support of this view will be adduced hereafter, and it is also most probably true that the choice of different or opposite vowels as exhibited in *qatil-yiqtal* and *qatal-yiqtul* was due to polarity (in so far as this term does not rather describe than explain a phenomenon), although it may be doubted whether this is the sole cause;[3] again, it seems indisputable that the permansive construction with nouns, as exhibited in the Acc. *šarrāku*, is as early as that with verbs, and indeed it may be suspected that it is the earlier of the two constructions. On the contrary, it is very difficult to follow him in supposing that the imperfect *yaqtul* and the imperative *qutul* are older than the permansive *qatil*, partly for reasons connected with inflection[4] and partly because it seems *a priori* likely that forms descriptive of facts are more primitive than those expressing modes. At the same time it is inconceivable that a preterite and a jussive form, however close the resemblance may be

[1] Meinhof, *Sprachen der Hamiten*, 151, 209 (cited by Bergsträsser).
[2] Meinhof, *op. cit.* 117 (cited by Bergsträsser).
[3] S. pp. 63–67.
[4] S. p. 28.

externally,[1] can have a common origin or indeed be in any way connected with one another; for strong asseveration cannot be regarded as an effective link between the two ideas, since the description of a past event differs in kind *toto caelo* from a command which in its very essence relates to future time, and the assumption that *yaqtul* was originally timeless and therefore universal lacks other support. Again, while the mere antiquity of *yaqtul* may be held to be proved by its wide diffusion in the Hamitic languages, it does not follow that it is older than *qatil*; for against this argument may be set the fact that Egyptian has nothing corresponding with *yaqtul* while it has a pseudo-participle of great antiquity corresponding closely with *qatil*.[2] Finally, the explanation of the Hebrew construction of consecutive *wāw* with the perfect, as brought into being as a kind of counterpoise to that of consecutive *wāw* with the imperfect, implies an artificiality of too conscious a kind to be really credible at an early stage in the development of language.

It may be added that Haupt,[3] who regards *yaqata/il* as primitive and *yaqtul* as the form next in order of development, advances yet other reasons for supposing *qati/al(a)* to be the latest form of the verb. These are: first, that the identity of vowels in the perfect as against the variety of them in the imperfect of all the themes of the Arabic verb is a mark of late schematization; second, that the forms of the perfect in the VIIth and VIIIth and Xth Arabic themes can be explained only if they are derived from the imperfect (for example, that *inqatala* must come from *yanqatilu*, as otherwise it must have been *naqatala*[4]); third, that the Accadian permansive *qaṭil* shows greater power of originality in creating new forms (such as *kabtāku* 'I am heavy,' *šarrāku* 'I am king,' *išāku* 'I have') than the Semitic perfect *qatal*, so that it cannot be a survival of it but must be an entirely different form; fourth, that Accadian seems never to have possessed and cannot therefore have lost a perfect *qaṭal*. To these reasons it may be

[1] Cp. S. R. Driver, *Tenses*, § 69.

[2] It is nothing but a *petitio principii* to argue that Egyptian once had a tense of the form *yaqtul*, since there are no traces of it in the language as now known; and, even if such a tense did once exist, that it has died out while the pseudo-participle has survived is no evidence that the former was older than the latter. Indeed, Zimmern (*V.G.S.S.* 94, 103) remarks that Hamitic forms are no safe guide in deciding the question of the relative priority of the various Semitic tense-forms, as Egyptian has only afformative and Kushite only preformative inflections, while Berber has a tense-form exhibiting a mixed inflection; and Bergsträsser (in *O. Lz.* XXVI. 257 [1]) similarly protests against comparing Bedawe or Hamitic forms, as there is no evidence whether they are proto-Semitic or have been newly created in the individual languages in which they occur.

[3] In *J.R.A.S.*, N.S. X. 244–51.

[4] Like Acc. *naqṭulu* and Hebr. *niqṭ*ᵉ*lû*; cp. Pal. *naqṣapu* (Knudtzon *A.-T.* 82, 51).

answered that the argument from uniformity or diversity of form may cut both ways,[1] that the so-called originality of the Acc. *qaṭil* is merely a matter of origin, and that the assertion that Accadian can never have had a perfect *qaṭal*, however likely it may be, begs the question. Brünnow[2] adds as yet another reason for considering *qati/ul* and *qatal* to be the latest forms that, while *yaqtul* with its prefixed pronouns has ceased to undergo development, the affixed formation exhibited by these has continued to spread in the new Semitic languages, being found not only in the old Accadian permansive forms but also in the new Syriac participial constructions; for a still living mode of formation is younger than one which has become entirely stereotyped. The Syr. *qāṭel-(')nâ* 'I am killing' is indeed the latest of all constructions exhibited by the Semitic verb, but that it has any necessary connection with the Acc. *qaṭlāku* 'I have (been), am killed' remains to be proved; in fact, several arguments tell against such a view. First, it uses in the first and third persons totally different forms or parts of the pronoun; second, it is demonstrably a crasis from the full Aram. *qāṭēl 'ᵉnâ*, which is found in the earlier Aramaic (and Syriac) dialects,[3] resulting naturally from the Semitic tendency to put the predicate before the subject and the Aramaic fondness for using the participle in place of a finite verb;[4] third, similar crases are common in Syriac, so that this particular instance can most easily be explained equally with them as a new and peculiar idiom developed within that language without any reference to past formations.

Philippi[5] follows Haupt in his attempt to separate the Acc. *qáṭil* from the Hebr. *qāṭál* on the additional grounds that the accentuation of the former does not, like that of the latter, agree with that of the perfect tense in the other Semitic languages and that, as it is joined with personal endings exactly as nouns may be, it is therefore a noun of the form *qátil* or *qātil*. The argument from the accentuation, however, can hardly be regarded as valid. For Beer[6] has rightly drawn attention to the fact that the Hebr. *qāṭᵉlāh* (and *qāṭᵉlû*) is accented archaistically, namely as the Acc. *qáṭlat* (and *qáṭlū*), and so shows that these forms are connected and, if this is so,

[1] S. pp. 15–16.
[2] In *Z.A.* VIII. 132[1].
[3] Cp. Schulthess, *Gramm. d. chr.-pal. Aram.* § 28.
[4] S. p. 27. Ewald (*Lehrb. d. hebr. Spr.* 437) thinks that the predicative use of the participle (except in circumstantial clauses) is of Aramaic origin (cp. Brockelmann, *G.V.G.S.S.* II. § 84 b). Similarity of idiom does not necessarily imply identity of origin; for example, the prepositions *l-* and *b-* seem both to be prefixed to the imperfect tense of the verb with different forces and at different periods in the development of the Semitic languages (s. p. 41), but there can be no connection between the two formations.
[5] In *B.A.S.S.* II. 371[2].
[6] In *Z.A.* XXXIV. 55–56.

it seems that there must be the same connection between the Acc. *qátil* and the Hebr. *qāṭál* in spite of the difference of accent; this then must be accented on the last syllable simply in conformity with the Hebrew rules of accentuation. Indeed, if diversity of accentuation indicated diversity of origin, it would be necessary to separate the Aram. *qᵉṭal* and the Syr. *qṭal* and the Eth. *qatála* from the Arab. *qátala* in spite of the identity of meaning; and this is absurd. The truth, then, seems to be that the accentuation of a form is a matter not of fundamental distinction but of dialectical peculiarity.[1] At the same time, the identity of the Accadian permansive *qaṭil* on the one side with a nominal or adjectival *qatil* (but not with a participial *qātil*, if only because a long vowel is never found in the permansive form) is not excluded by a connection on the other side with a perfect *qatal*. In fact, Knudtzon[2] argues that *i* and not *a* is the original vowel of *qatal* on the grounds that those Hebrew verbs which preserve the present significance of the form have mostly *ē* or *ō* going back respectively to *i* or *u* and that the participle is *qōṭēl* which derives from an original *qātil* (of which he finds traces in the Hebr. *bōḵîyāh* 'weeping' and in the Aramaic participle *qāṭil* beside *qāṭēl*), being also an offshoot of *qatil*; moreover, the change of *i* into *a* is no uncommon phenomenon.[3] It is therefore safe to assume that a primitive *qatil* lies not only behind verbs descriptive of states but also behind those expressing activity. Further, Poebel[4] rightly finds an argument for such a connection in the numerous instances in which the Acc. *qaṭil* has the same force as the Hebr. *qāṭal*, notably in such verbs as *maḫir* 'he has received' and indeed in many other verbs; consequently the change of vocalization seems to be not the mark of an originally independent verbal form but the result of this extension of meaning in an originally nominal or adjectival form. Nor have combinations of noun and pronominal element (such as *šarrāku* 'I am king') any real evidential value in this connection; for the comparative rarity of their occurrence and the fact that they are almost confined to terms denoting title or dignity suggest that they are not a normal construction but are rather an artificial extension of the combination of primitive noun or adjective and pronoun invented for a special purpose, *i.e.* the glorification of various exalted personages.

At the same time, Knudtzon[5] shows that the permansive and perfect forms are identifiable also in respect to their functions.

[1] Cp. Acc. *iqṭul* with Hebr. *yiqṭōl* (s. pp. 88–91).
[2] In *Z.A.* VII. 43–46.
[3] Cp. Brockelmann, *G.V.G.S.S.* I. § 52 g.
[4] In *O. Lz.* XIX. 47–48 (cp. Acc. *nadin*=Hebr. *nāṯan* 'he has given').
[5] In *Z.A.* VII. 33–48.

Originally both described a neutral state, and all their functions can be subsumed 'under the conception of the actual' or 'present.'[1] What, however, is actual or present is also 'what is completed' or 'brought to a close,'[2] which is often described by the Semitic perfect, and so past events are frequently described by it (as also by the permansive, though rarely owing to the development of a preterite in Accadian). It might indeed be objected that the perfect is in no way related to the present significance but consists solely in the fact that it is the past which is stated or described, whence it might be inferred that first the perfect and second the present significance of the perfect-permansive form was evolved. This, however, is not so; for, for example, the perfect in 'the heavens are higher (*gāḇᵉhû*) than the earth'[3] means not that the heavens have become but that they are higher than the earth. This form therefore does not necessarily describe 'a state which has arisen'[4] out of something antecedent; in fact, it often describes not 'an actual result, the conclusion of a process, something which has occurred,'[5] but 'something existent, actual,' or 'present.'[6] On the one hand, this agrees with the fact that an adjective often coexists with these permansive-perfect forms (such as the Acc. *kabtu*=Hebr. *kāḇēḏ* 'heavy' beside the Acc. *kabit*= Hebr. *kāḇēḏ* 'is, was heavy'); for in adjectives no one thinks 'of a state which has come about' or 'occurred.'[7] In Accadian too, when the permansive has a predominantly present significance, its stem often appears as a noun, while adjectives commonly have permansive forms (such as *qaṭi/ul* and *quṭṭul*). On the other hand, the perfect is readily developed out of the present sense as 'he is clothed' easily passes into 'he has put on (clothes).' The transition of meaning is often clear: for example, in 'thou art wiser (*ḥāḵam 'attā*) than Daniel'[8] the reference is to a present state, while in 'if thou hadst been wise (*ḥāḵamtā*), thou hadst been wise (*ḥāḵamtā*) to thyself'[9] a particular state in past time is taken as typical of a general or universal condition, so that 'if thou art wise, thou art wise to thyself,' comes to be a fair rendering of the Hebrew saying. Moreover, the proper perfect does not immediately describe 'something which, being completed or closed, is actual' or 'present,'[10] as the Gk. προκεχώρηκα 'I have advanced' or προκέκοφα 'I have pro-

[1] Germ. *unter dem Begriffe des Vorliegenden.*
[2] Germ. *das Vollendete, Abgeschlossene.*
[3] Is. *55*. 9.
[4] Germ. *einen eingetretenen Zustand.*
[5] Germ. *ein vorliegendes Ergebnis, den Abschluss eines Werdens, etwas Eingetretenes.*
[6] Germ. *etwas Vorhandenes, Vorliegendes.*
[7] Germ. *an einen eingetretenen Zustand.*
[8] Ezek. *28*. 3.
[9] Prov. *9*. 12.
[10] Germ. *etwas vollendet oder abgeschlossen Vorliegendes.*

gressed ' can have such a meaning when the advance or progress is not complete in the eyes of the speaker; in such cases it describes ' something which has happened, something which has come about, which is actual ' or ' present,'[1] and thus an actual fact is stated or asserted. Lastly, the passive use of the same form, common in Accadian but rare in Hebrew,[2] arose as easily as ' to be full ' passes over into ' to be filled,' when the state so described was brought about by some external agency; such a passive use, however, can occur only with a perfect or pluperfect force. The eventual identity therefore of *qatil* and *qatal*, whatever the order of their development may be, cannot be denied.

Again, Ahrens[3] finds an argument for the priority of *yaqtul* over against *qatil* from the existence of apocopated forms in certain classes of weak verbs as set out in the following table:

Pf.	Consec. Impf.	Juss.	Impt.
yālaḏ	*wayyēleḏ*	*yēlēḏ*	*lēḏ*
rāḇāh	*wayyireḇ*	*yireḇ*	—
sāḇaḇ	*wayyāsōḇ*	*yāsōḇ*	*sōb*
nāṯan	*wayyittēn*	*yittēn*	*tēn*

He argues then from this table that the consecutive imperfect and jussive and imperative forms are biliteral, while those of the perfect tense are triliteral, and that therefore the latter is later in development than any of the former, since the course of development in the Semitic languages has been not from triliteral to biliteral but from biliteral to triliteral forms. This fact is indeed almost certainly true,[4] but the argument as here applied is far from being sound for a number of reasons. First, the forms here postulated do not run uniformly throughout the Semitic languages (for example, the Acc. *šalālu* makes only *išlul*, and the Acc. *rabū* makes only *irbi* in the preterite tense, and so, too, the Arab. *salla* makes only an imperative *sull*); second, many types of shortening in the Semitic languages are demonstrably secondary (for example, in the Bab. *irab* for *irabbi*, while the dated Aramaic papyri prove that the Aram. *yintēn* is older than *yittēn*); third, even amongst verbs with initial *w*- or *y*- many preserve clear traces of the original weak consonant (for example, the Acc. *ešīru* makes imperative *ešir* and the Hebr. *yāšar* makes imperfect *yiyšar*>*yīšar*). It is therefore obvious that no importance can be attached to these apocopated forms; few occur alike in all the Semitic languages, many if not all are equally easily explained as due to shortening as to lengthening, even though all Semitic verbs

[1] Germ. *etwas Geschehenes, etwas Eingetretenes, das vorliegt.*
[2] Cp. Hebr. *mālē'* ' was full, was filled; filled ' (s. p. 52).
[3] In *Z.D.M.G.* LXIV. 189–190.
[4] S. pp. 5–6.

may have originally been biliteral and not triliteral, within the period of historical development. The argument therefore from the apocopated forms, being ambiguous, proves nothing.

Finally, Knudtzon [1] thinks that the imperfect is prior to the permansive-perfect on the ground that it is natural for 'something presenting itself' [2] to the observation to be expressed before 'that which is actual' or 'present'; [3] for the former offers itself to or immediately forces itself upon a man's notice and rouses his attention, while the latter so far from doing this must make a greater effort to impress itself on him and requires more independent activity on the part of the mind and more reflection. This argument rests on the assumption that human beings began by observing in the first instance what most forcibly drew their attention and then went on to look at the accompanying circumstances; but reflection seems to show that in actual fact a man only sees what comes towards him as it arises out of a background which he has already observed.

Although, then, all these scholars maintain the view that either *yaqtul* or *qutul* is the original form of the Semitic verb, it is difficult to agree with them not only for the negative reasons already brought against it but also because it seems possible to adduce positive arguments which appear to be cogent in favour of the priority of *qati/ul* and thereafter of *qatal*.

Thus Hommel,[4] in the first place, argues that priority of *qati/ul* over against *qatal* is proved by the fact that *i* or *u* rather than *a* is the primitive vowel of this form; for it has maintained itself also in the Arab. *qumtu* (<*qaumtu*) and *ṣirtu* (<*ṣairtu*) and *nimtu* (<*naimtu*) [5] beside *qâma* and *sâra* and *nâma*, and that *a* and *i* represent a primary vocalization agrees with the vocalization of *yaqûmu* and *yasîru* (whereas *yanâmu* shows a secondary form of vocalization). At the same time, the Eth. *qōma* and *mēta* agree with the vocalization of *qumtu* against that of *qâma*, and so on, thus confirming the view that *u* and *i* are the original vowels. So too König [6] argues with much force that there is some evidence that *u* is the proper intransitive or passive vowel (for example, in the Hebr. *qāṭûl* and the Arab. *maqṭûl*^{un}, to which may be added the passive forms of the various verbal themes), so that the perfect *qatul* is likely to be primitive rather than the imperfect *yaqtal* which corresponds with it. In the second place Hommel,[7] following Lagarde, draws another proof from the meaning of these forms, and he takes as his examples on the one hand the Arabic *kabura*

[1] In *Z.A.* VII. 58.
[2] Germ. *etwas sich Darstellendes.*
[3] Germ. *das Vorliegende.*
[4] In *Z.D.M.G.* XLIV. 540–541.
[5] Cp. *nimru* (<*namiru*) 'panther.'
[6] In *Z.D.M.G.* LXV. 720.
[7] In *Z.D.M.G.* XLIV. 536–537.

'he is big' and *yabisa* 'he is dry (but may become wet),' and on the other hand *kataba* 'he writes.' Thus he sees in *kabura* 'a statement concerning an experience, an impression,'[1] and in *yabisa* 'a statement concerning a representation or description —that is, recollections of an experience, an impression, or an anticipation of such, in which already reflection plays a part.'[2] In other words, forms describing a permanent or unchangeable state are antecedent to those applied to the description of temporary states, since the use of such forms necessitates reflection in order to realize that the state so described is changeable. Lastly *kataba* describes something that the speaker has previously seen; and to reflect as well as to relate and to compare are the predominating marks of a later age, while naïve and unconscious experience, resting on immediate impression and the description of the known, become ever more characteristic of the earlier period the further back one goes.[3]

In the first place, too, the uninflected *qatil* (with *qutul*, of which something will be said hereafter) is on the surface the simplest form of the verb from which all other forms have been demonstrably developed; and analogy suggests that what is simplest is earliest, as the Greek present is certainly prior to the future and aorist tenses. Second, the fact that in Accadian nouns and adjectives can be inflected in the same way as verbs in the permansive state, so that it may at times be impossible to say whether any given form is a noun or a verb (*e.g.* whether *šaknāku* means 'I am' or 'have been appointed' or 'I am an appointee'), shows that *qatil* goes back to a very early period of time when the noun or adjective on the one hand and the verb on the other hand were still but imperfectly distinguished;[4] and this impression is strengthened by the fact that *qatil* exhibits a mixed inflection, purely nominal and primitive in the third person but developed and pseudo-verbal in the second and first persons.[5] If, then, the uninflected *qatil* is prior to

[1] Germ. *eine Aussage über eine Empfindung, ein Eindruck.*

[2] Germ. *eine Aussage über eine Vorstellung, d.h. die Erinnerungen einer Empfindung, einen Eindruck, oder Vorahnung eines solchen, wobei schon die Reflexion mitspielt.*

[3] Germ. *in je frühere Zeit wir zurückgehen, die naive und unbewusste, auf unmittelbaren Eindruck beruhende, Empfindung und Vorstellung des Kundes dem Reflectiren, Referiren und vollens Vergleichen des reiferen Alters gegenüber vorwiegen wird.*

[4] Words derived from the permansive state, though construed as nouns capable of governing the genitive case (as in *šakni ša Esaggil* 'governor of E.'), generally took the adjectival plural ending *-ūtu*, and were followed by prepositions (as in *ša . . . šaknūti elišunu ištakanu* 'who . . . appointed governors over them'); sometimes they took both the adjectival plural ending *-ūtu* and the nominal plural ending *-āni* (for example, from *qīp* 'was entrusted' is formed *qīpu* 'entrusted' = 'officer entrusted with a charge,' of which the plural forms are both *qīpūtu* and *qīpāni*). Thus it remained to the end uncertain whether such words were nouns or adjectives.

[5] Nyberg (in *M. Or.* XIV. 187–188) draws attention to the fact that *qatal* is not yet fully admitted into the verbal system but is still rather a participle or *nomen agentis*, as its function shows.

the inflected second and first persons, it seems that it must also be prior to the inflected *yaqtul*, and it is then natural to suppose that all the parts of *qatil* must have preceded all those of *yaqtul*, which must have come into existence practically at the same moment of time. Third, it seems likely that a form with an afformative is older than one with a preformative inflection, since it conforms to a general rule of the Semitic languages that the predicate precedes the subject if the emphasis rests on it or if the subject is a pronoun which is *per se* unemphatic [1]; in this case the subject, when expressed, is a pronoun, and the emphasis clearly rests on *qatil* which is the essential element in the combination. Fourth, on the one hand the pronominal affixes show forms more primitive because less worn away than those of the prefixes. On the other hand, if the prefixed *y*- is a weakened fragment of the -*w*- [2] which appears as a basal element of the pronoun of the third person in most of the Semitic languages, time must be allowed for the process of attrition and coalescence, and the combined form must be subsequent in point of development to its component parts. Fifth, the difficult prefix *ta*-, expressing the feminine third person in *taqatal* and *taqtul*, is only explicable as having arisen out of *qat*(*i*)*lat* (where it is a nominal ending) [3] on the false analogy of the prefix *ta*- expressing the masculine second person in *taqtul*, in the same way as the *n*- of the plural first person has been transferred, so to say, from the end of *qatalnā* to the beginning of *naqtul*. So, too, the plural ending -*ū* in *yaqatalū* and *yaqtulū* can be explained only as having arisen through the false analogy of the permansive plural *qat*(*i*)*lū* and not *vice versa*; yet there it is nothing else than the termination of a plural noun (as found in several of the Semitic languages [4]) which, though properly attached to a nominal, is strictly inappropriate to a verbal form. Again, the sole assumption which will account for the subjunctive ending -*u* is that it was originally a nominal ending proper to the permansive *qatil* and that it was subsequently applied by false analogy to the other tenses when they were evolved.[5] These arguments indeed are formally conclusive, since the endings -*at* in *qat*(*i*)*lat* and -*ū* in *qat*(*i*)*lū* cannot be explained as having owed their

[1] S. p. 21. So the Hebrew rule is that the predicate must precede the subject when it is emphatic and may precede it when the subject is a pronoun, since 'the person assumed to be known does not excite the same interest as that which is stated about him' (Kautzsch & Cowley, *Hebr. Gramm.* § 141 n); rules similar to those in force in Hebrew are found also in Aramaic, Arabic and Ethiopic (Brockelmann, *G.V.G.S.S.* II. § 47 b–e).

[2] S. pp. 38–39. [3] S. pp. 39–40.

[4] The old Babylonian -*ū* and the Arabic -*ūna* (-*ū*) alone exhibit this ending in full use.

[5] S. pp. 75–77.

origin to *taqtul* and *yaqtulu* respectively,[1] nor can the subjunctive -*u* be explained if *qatil* is younger than *yaqtul*(*u*).[2] Sixth, the uses to which *qatil* is put are of almost universal range, as numerous examples testify,[3] and these must reflect a period of time antecedent to the development of *yaqatal* and *yaqtul* which both have a strictly limited reference; for, indeed, it is hardly conceivable that subsequently to the evolution of these two tenses another neutral form of universal application overlapping them can either have grown up or been created.

Hommel,[4] again following Lagarde, holds that the imperative *qutul* is antecedent to the permansive *qatu/il* and the perfect *qatal* because it is recognized in many primitive nouns: for example, the Arab. *'iṣbaʿ*^{un} 'finger' is derived from the imperative *iṣbaʿ* 'point.'[5] For naturally the oldest nouns are those which owe their origin to the wish of the child or to the antecedent wish of its parents; thus many proper names are of imperatival form. He also finds it significant that the imperative and infinitive forms, such as the Hebr. *qᵉṭōl* 'kill' and 'to kill,' are often identical. The latter fact is hardly of much significance in this connection; the former, granted that it is true in the case cited, is true only of certain languages and so is not sufficient to prove the case. On the contrary, it is probably necessary to regard the imperative *qutul* as posterior in time of development to the permansive *qatil* as also is the jussive *yaqtul* to the preterite tense; for not only are there traces of the permansive even in the second person performing the function of an imperative, which it would hardly have taken over if there had already been an imperative in use, but also the -*u* in the plural second person can only be explained as being derived by false analogy through the preterite from the permansive, since it is of nominal origin, while the jussive has clearly been inflected on the analogy of the preterite.

It would seem *a priori* likely that primitive man would be occupied rather with present and future than with past events, *i.e.* with the needs of daily life rather than with history, and it would therefore be natural to expect that, so soon as the ambiguities of the universal usage of *qatil* came to be felt, the first requirement of the early Semites would be a present-future tense; and that *qatil* expressed properly state, which

[1] The Semitic languages have no feminine singular pronoun of the third person containing a *t*; for in the Eth. *we'etū* 'he' and *ye'etī* 'she' the pronominal elements are respectively *w*- and *y*-, and the -*t*- is merely deictic (s. pp. 36–37, 38–40).

[2] S. pp. 75–77.

[3] S. pp. 113–118.

[4] In *Z.D.M.G.* XLIV. 537–538.

[5] So the Acc. *ṣumb*^{um} (originally *ṣubb*^{um} $<$ *ṣubʿ*^{um}) 'finger' is of imperatival form.

had of necessity arisen in time already past at the moment of speaking, would make the need of a present-future more urgent than that of a preterite tense. So the Greek language appears to have evolved first a present and second a future before any past tense ; for already in Homer the future forms of the verb are clearly marked, while the sole sign of a past tense, namely the augment, is optional (as indeed it remains to the end in the pluperfect tense). At the same time the equivocal nature of *qatil*, which was in accordance with its origin predominantly intransitive but was almost necessarily at times used in a transitive sense, made it inevitable that the new tense should be active in meaning.

These arguments, although they suggest that the immediate need of the proto-Semitic speech was a present-future tense with an active significance, are more or less subjective, but they can be reinforced by another of a purely objective nature derived from the formal evolution of the new tense. It may now be presumed that such a form as *qátil-ta*, in which the nominal or verbal precedes the pronominal element, is already in existence, and it will be conceded that the obvious and indeed only possible way of creating a new form out of the same given elements is to invert them ; of this process *ta-qáta/il*[1] is the result. Accordingly Hommel,[2] observing that the accent in both forms falls in the same place, argues convincingly for an immediate connection between them, whereas the accentuation of *yáqtul* shows that it cannot be connected directly with *qátu/il*.[3] Again, as *qátil-ta* and *ta-qáta/il* are formally so close to one another, so their meanings overlap in so far as both at bottom mean 'thou (art in a) killing (state)' ; but, while *qátilta* clung naturally to those meanings which predominated with the old *qátil*, namely to the expression of states arising in the past and continuing into the present, the new *taqáta/il* took over that sphere which *qátil* occupied only by an extension of its proper function, namely the description of present and future time. It may also be worth remarking that Haupt,[4] arguing that it cannot be accidental that Accadian and Ethiopic have each devised a tense with an accented middle syllable, especially as these two languages

[1] The varieties of vocalization have here no significance (s. pp. 56–57).

[2] In *Z.D.M.G.* XLIV. 538–540.

[3] The Acc. *qáṭlū* as against the Aram. *qᵉṭálû* suggests that the accent in the primitive form fell rather on the first than the second syllable ; and the Hebrew accentuation of the perfect tense with consecutive *wāw* accords with this suggestion (s. pp. 88–90).

[4] In *J.R.A.S.*, N.S. X. 245–248. It may, however, be doubted whether Haupt is right in further arguing that the Eth. *yeqtel* is derived from *yeqatel* as the Acc. *iqṭul* is from *iqaṭa/il*, since *yeqṭel* is probably an independent form like (*l*)*iqṭul* (s. p. 35).

have a number of other common peculiarities, infers that the Acc. *iqáṭil*=the Eth. *yeqátel* must go back to the common archetype of the Semitic speech and therefore be the primitive tense-form.

Lastly comes reflection upon past events, and so it is reasonable to suppose that the development of the preterite followed that of the present-future tense; and this too can be formally proved. Starting from the fact that in *qátilta* an afformative and in *taqáta/il* a preformative conjugation already existed and given once again the same data, the sole course now open for the creation of a third tense was by the modification of one of these forms. Negatively, it is difficult to see how *yáqtul* can have arisen directly out of *qátil* in view of the position of the accent in the two forms. Positively, the fact that *taqáta/il* is not a form partly nominal and partly verbal describing a state but a proper tense expressing something of the same nature as that which the latest form is required to express, namely activity, shows why it was preferred for modification; thus the new form has prefixed, not postfixed, inflections. Knudtzon [1] has therefore rightly seen that *yáqtul* is derived from *yaqátil* through the elision of its medial vowel even though it bears the accent; [2] but this phenomenon is not unparalleled in the Semitic languages.[3] Thus it seems that *yáqtul* is posterior in time to *yaqátil*, if only for the reasons given above. So too Beer [4] argues that *yaqtúl* certainly went back to an older *yáqtul*, since *ya*+*qutul* (or rather *ya*+*qatil*) could only have become *yaqtul* through the loss of the middle vowel if the prefix was originally accented, and accordingly he is able to show that the preterite forms are old while the imperfect forms are a new formation, since they (for example, the Hebr. *wayyā̊qom* and *wayyā̊qem*) retain the old accentuation of the prefix. Moreover, this argument agrees with the fact that such lengthening in consequence of accentuating a final syllable (for example, in the Hebr. *hiqṭîl* as compared with the Syr. *'aqṭel* and the Arab. *'aqtala*) is a peculiarly Hebrew and therefore relatively late phenomenon. At the same time Knudtzon [5] has suggested two other reasons in favour of this view, and they may be briefly stated here. These are that the diverse uses of the Acc. *iqaṭal* and the Eth. *yeqatel* argue great antiquity, and that forms like *yaqata/il*

[1] In *Z.A.* VII. 49–50.

[2] Barth (in *Z.A.* II. 376–378) will not allow that the Acc. *iqaṭal* and *iqṭul* are connected in view of the difference in the vowels, but the reason is hardly cogent when the probable causes of the variation in the vocalization of these forms are considered (s. pp. 53–54, 57–58, 60–62).

[3] The Accadian infinitive *itappuṣu* (=*itápuṣu*)>*itpuṣu* illustrates this elision of an accented vowel, which is by no means rare (Delitzsch, *Ass. Gramm.* 259*).

[4] In *Z.At.W.* XXXIV. 55–56.

[5] In *Z.A.* VI. 420–421.

describing what is actually (externally) present [1] must be regarded as prior to those expressing what is appearing (whether from outside or within) to a person as coming into being and is only to that extent something present,[2] such as the W.-Semitic imperfect tense as seen in the Hebr. *yiqṭōl* describes.[3]

[1] Germ. *wirklich* (*aüsserlich*) *Gegenwärtiges.*

[2] Germ. *das sich Jemandem* (*aüsserlich oder innerlich*) *Darstellende, Hervortretende, also etwas Gegenwärtiges.*

[3] Knudtzon (in *Z.A.* VI. 419–422) also argues that *yaqtul* is posterior to *yaqata/il*, on the ground that the Eth. *yeqtel* has only a subjunctive use ; but there are reasons for doubting whether *yaqtul* (whether a preterite or an imperfect tense) is connected with the Eth. *yeqtel* (s. p. 35).

IV

ORIGIN OF IMPERATIVE AND JUSSIVE FORMS

THE analogy of other languages, as for example the Latin *fac* and *dic* show, suggests that the shortest possible form of the verb will be required for the expression of a command; for thus an abrupt tone will be given to it. Accordingly, it is natural to find that the Semitic imperative form in its simplest state consists of the radical consonants without any preformative or afformative element; but it is distinguished from the simplest form of the permansive state, with which it is otherwise externally identical, by two things, namely the position of the accent and the nature of the vowels. In the statement of a fact for which the permansive state is used, it is necessary to give full weight to the root which predicates something of the subject, and so the accent is laid on the first syllable of this form, thereby holding the speaker back and keeping the stress on the emphatic word; the abruptness of a command on the contrary is indicated by his hurrying on to the last syllable, which thus receives the accent, while the first syllable is almost if not quite unsounded.[1] Consequently, the first vowel, which was of little importance except as a helping vowel, was simply assimilated to the second vowel, and this was generally if not always determined in the same way as the vowel of *yaqtul*: thus were formed the Acc. *kušud* (*ikšud*), *piqid* (*iqpid*), *limad* (*ilmad*), *ṣabat* (*iṣbat*).[2] Although, however, the second vowel of the imperative form is identical with that of the preterite tense, it must not be supposed that the former follows or is based on the later, since there are insuperable semantic objections to connecting these two forms; the identity is due merely to the

[1] Bauer & Leander (*Hist. Gr. d. hebr. Spr.* I. 304–305) put the accent on the first syllable of the Acc. *quṭul* in view of the loss of the vowel in the second syllable in such forms as *quṭlū*. This, however, can hardly be right; for the fact that the first vowel was determined by the second vowel shows that it was of no importance. Moreover, this suggestion is confirmed by the other Semitic languages, in which such forms as the Hebr. *meˡlôḵî* (in so far as they are correctly transmitted) and the classical Arab. *uktub* (which has given place to the modern Arab. *ktûb*), point to a proto-Sem. *qutúlū* accented like the Eth. *qetélū*; and, lastly, the uncertainty about the vocalization of the first syllable in many Hebrew imperatives (*ibid.* 306) is clearly due to the lack of importance of this vowel. If this argument is correct, the Acc. *quṭlū* has arisen out of the proto-Sem. *qutúlū* in the same way as *itápuṣu* becomes *itpuṣu* by the elision of an accented vowel (s. p. 30).

[2] In imperatives of the form *qital* (such as *limad, pilaḫ, rikab*) the *i* is due to the proximity of the liquid *l* or *r* as the case may be (s. pp. 55–56).

application of the same principles, whatever these may be, in the determination of the vowel in both cases.[1]

Hitherto there has not been found a satisfactory solution of this difficulty of the Semitic verbal system, namely why *yaqtul* has not only a preterite sense but also a jussive or precative as well as a present-future significance. The problem is raised in its simplest form in Accadian and may at the outset be discussed solely with reference to that language. There *ikšud* means 'he captured'; but how can *likšud* (< *lū ikšud*) mean both 'he surely captured' and 'let him capture,' and how can the same form underlie both *ūl* (*lā*) *ikšud* 'he did not capture' and *ai ikšud* 'let him not capture'?[2] Semantically it is impossible to see any connection between these usages; it is impossible to conceive any transition of sense whereby *ikšud* meaning 'he captured' (for Accadian usage shows clearly that the preterite tense in no sense can be said to denote nascent or emergent action, in spite of attempts to prove the contrary)[3] can have come to mean also 'let him capture,' or *vice versa*. The only way out of this difficulty is to assume that the preterite *ikšud* is formally independent of the jussive or precative *ikšud* and that it has arisen spontaneously from a different origin.[4] The analogy of Latin shows that an imperative mood containing only a second person was inadequate; for it is but a step from a command in the second person to an 'exhortation' in the third person[5] with which almost simultaneously arises the need for 'cohortation' in the first person. So the first and third person of the subjunctive mood were pressed into use, especially in negative clauses, to supplement its deficiencies, and indeed it was no long time before the latter, which expressed a milder and more polite form of dissuasion, ousted the former in prohibitions in the third person. Accordingly, Ungnad[6] is probably right in regarding the jussive first and third persons as extensions of the imperative second person. The inadequacy of the imperative *qutúl* in the second

[1] S. pp. 53–61.

[2] Bauer (in *B.A.S.S.* VIII. i. 20–21) explains the use of the same form in such diverse constructions by referring it back to a time when *iqṭul* was still universal and had not yet developed a preterite sense; but such a theory seems to raise as many difficulties as it removes, if only because there is no direct evidence of such a use of this form (s. pp. 10, 19–20).

[3] S. pp. 108–110, 120–121, 125–128.

[4] Such identity of form with diversity of origin is no cause for surprise, being commonly found also in Indo-European languages; thus the two Lat. *legimini* 'you are gathered' and 'be ye gathered' are derived from different sources, the first being the Gk. λεγόμενοι 'being gathered,' and the second the Gk. λεγεμέναι 'to be gathered' (Giles, *Manual of Comparative Philology*, 360, 388).

[5] So the Gk. λεγόντων=the Lat. *legunto* 'let them be gathered' are generally held to be comparatively late creations (Giles, *op. cit.* 25).

[6] In *B.A.S.S.* V. 249–250.

person gave rise to a jussive *ya-qutúl* and a cohortative *a-qutúl* formed by prefixing the necessary pronominal elements; and these by the loss of the unstressed vowel in the first syllable of *qutúl* became respectively *yáqtul* and *áqtul*, in which the accent has been thrown back on to the pronominal elements in accordance with the proto-Semitic rules regulating the free accent.[1] It is this fact which accounts for the existence of the apocopated jussive forms which Philippi [2] is therefore without doubt wrong in regarding as primitive; moreover, they occur only in certain languages, namely in Hebrew and Aramaic and Arabic, and in these only in certain verbs of a single class. The reason why the pronominal elements were prefixed in the precative form derived from the imperative *qutul* was not merely imitation of or assimilation to the preterite *yaqtul*, but also that the almost unsounded vowel in the first and the stress on the second syllable would have further withdrawn the sound from the beginning of the word and made the resultant form almost unpronounceable; further, the third and first persons as distinct from the second person (which is virtually implied in all imperative forms and is therefore left unexpressed in most languages) required to be emphasized and so was put first to draw attention to it. Precative forms, however, are in themselves to a certain extent emphatic, and so there grew up at any rate in Accadian the custom of prefixing the affirmative particle *lū* 'verily' (or sometimes the cohortative *ī*) to these forms. In the same way this particle is often though not always employed with the permansive state when it is desired to make its optative force clear. Simultaneously, this particle served to distinguish the precative *ikšud* from the preterite *ikšud*; but the fact that *lū* was not properly precative but affirmative in meaning resulted in the possibility of prefixing it also to the preterite *ikšud* and consequently (*lū ikšud* >) *likšud* could mean either 'let him seize' or 'surely he seized.' Thus its distinguishing purpose proved abortive, but in practice the context made it clear which sense was intended, just as in a letter there can be no doubt that *lū šalmāku* as said by the sender means 'verily I am well,' while *lū šalmāta* as said to the receiver means 'mayst thou verily be well.'[3] So, too, in Hebrew the enclitic *nâ* is sometimes attached to the precative to distinguish it from the preterite-imperfect *yiqṭōl*, but its frequent omission shows that the context here, too, was generally sufficient to decide which sense or rather which form was intended.

[1] Cp. Bauer & Leander, *Hist. Gr. d. hebr. Spr.* I. 177.

[2] In *B.A.S.S.* II. 376†.

[3] This particle is once attached to the perfect tense with consecutive *wāw* with precative force (Gen. *40*. 14), just as the Acc. *lū* is sometimes found with the permansive state when its force is optative.

Similarly, the Eth. *yeqtel*, which has both a jussive and a subjunctive force,[1] is probably connected with the precative Acc. *iqṭul* and the jussive Hebr. *yiqṭōl* and Arab. *yaqtul* rather than with the subjunctive Arab. *yaqtula*; for it can stand in independent as in dependent clauses, whereas the Arabic subjunctive seems to be a mere mode of the indicative *yaqtulu*[2] with which no form in Ethiopic corresponds.

[1] Dillmann & Crichton, *Eth. Gramm.* 173–174. [2] S. pp. 78–79.

One curious point here calls for comment. Accadian in the permansive state preserves the true distinction respectively in *qaṭlāk(u)* and *qaṭlāt(a)* between the first and second persons;[1] most of the other languages in the perfect tense have confused these pronominal elements, Arabic in agreement with Hebrew and Aramaic having *-t-* in both persons, as seen in *qataltu* 'I have killed' and *qatalta* 'thou hast killed,' and Ethiopic alone having *-k-* [2] in both persons, as in *qatalkū* 'I have killed' and *qatalka* 'thou hast killed.' The confusion is clearly due to the influence of analogy, possibly assisted by phonetic resemblance; for in Hebrew and Aramaic and Arabic the analogy of the second has affected the first person, and in Ethiopic that of the first has affected the second person, while the force of analogy has been reinforced by the affinity of *k* to *t*, as shown by the facility with which they may be interchanged in certain languages.[3] Thus these forms all go back to a period in which the first person will have had a *-k-* probably also in the independent pronoun, even though it has fallen away in the language as now known; for otherwise the forms with *-t-* in the first person are equally inexplicable.

The third persons, both singular and plural, of the preterite-imperfect tense have been the cause of much discussion. Dieterich [4] has argued that they too are of nominal origin and that in fact *yaqtul* and *taqtul* are two different types of abstract noun. It is however difficult to assume yet other nominal forms developed into a verb, and the fact that *yaqatal*, which must be regarded as a prior development and which is hardly explicable as being also of nominal origin,[5] if only because such a nominal formation is hardly known, exhibits the same inflexions, makes this view untenable. The old theory, therefore, which Gesenius [6] admitted, though with hesitation, that *y(a)-* is connected with the pronoun of the singular third pronoun must be re-examined. There is a common deictic *h* found in various Semitic particles, such as the Hebr. *hē'*, the Aram. *hâ* and the Arab. *hâ* 'lo!', and this cannot be separated from the Hebrew definite article [7] and the *ha-* in the Hebr. *hazzeh* [8]

[1] Knudtzon (in *Z.A.* VI. 418–419) is probably right in explaining the *-ā-* in *-(ā)kū* and *-(ā)tā* as analogous to the helping vowel in the first and second persons of the permansive-perfect forms of geminate verbs which in their turn owe them to the analogy of the verbs ending in a final weak consonant (s. Zimmern, *V.G.S.S.* § 50 e).

[2] This *-k-* is preserved also in the Sabæan dialect as also in Mehri and Socotri (Brockelmann, *G.V.G.S.S.* I. 573–574).

[3] Cp. Gk. τίς=Lat. *quis* and Gk. τέτταρες=Lat. *quattuor*, and so on (s. Zimmern, *V.G.S.S.* 22–23, who doubts this influence in view of the absence of any other instances of the interchange of *k* and *t* in the Semitic languages).

[4] In *Abh. z. hebr. Gramm.* 97 ff. (s. S. R. Driver, *Tenses*, 7–11).

[5] S. pp. 29–30.

[6] In *Lehrgeb. d. hebr. Spr.* 274–275.

[7] Cp. Sab. *hn* 'the'

[8] G. R. Driver in *J.T.S.* XXX. 377–378.

and *hallāzeh* 'this,' the Syr. *hau* 'that' and *hān* 'this' and the Arab. *hāḏâ* 'this.' This, then, also lies behind the early Aram. *hw*, the Hebr. *hû'* and the Arab. *huwa*, and these in turn are cognate with the Eth. *we'etū* (=*we'e*+*tū*) 'he';[1] the Phœn. *h* or *hy* (as Plautus wrote it) as well as the Mehr. *he*, *hi* 'he'[2] are also forms of this pronoun. At the same time the suffixed Aram. *-h* and the Hebr. *-h* (*-w*) must be compared with the Phœn. *-'* or *-y* 'him, his,' which is identical with the prefix of the same person in the imperfect tense. There is therefore evidence not only of a deictic *h* but also of this or a kindred element in course of transition from *w* to *y*[3] going to the composition of the pronoun of the third person; and the preference for *y-* as the verbal prefix is easily explained by the readiness with which these two weak letters were interchanged[4] and the well-known aversion of several Semitic languages to leaving *w-* at the beginning of a word. Consequently the old view that the prefixed *ya-* (=Acc. *i-* and Hebr. *yi-*) is connected with a deictic or demonstrative element in the pronoun of the singular third person may be accepted. The feminine singular form adopted the nominal *-(a)t* as *t(a)-* to indicate the feminine subject on the analogy of the pronominal elements of the second and first persons,[5] yet the analogy was not so false as it might seem at first sight to be, since there are clear traces of an initial *t-* serving as a feminine deictic or demonstrative element, for example, in certain feminine pronouns such as the Arab. *tâ* or *tī* and *hātī* 'this' and *tâka* or *tîka* and *tilka* 'that.'[6] The use of this feminine *t-* however seems not to be primary with verbs, being found very rarely in Old-Babylonian texts and only in reference to persons and not to things in Old-Assyrian texts;[7] this agrees with the fact that the need to distinguish the gender of persons is more necessary than that of signifying that

[1] Originally (*hu*)*we'*+*tū*. Whether the Acc. *šu'atu* 'he' is also cognate with these forms in view of a possible *š* / *s* > *h* > ' in the Semitic languages (cp. Zimmern, *V.G.S.S.* § 9 g) may be doubted (cp. Brockelmann, *G.V.G.S.S.* I. § 104, f β–γ).

[2] *Ibid.* δ.

[3] Cp. Philippi in *B.A.S.S.* II. 370 **. There may be another trace of this *y*- in the Arab. *yâ* 'oh!' and in *'îjâ-* or *hîyâ-* prefixed to pronominal suffixes, as in *'îyâhu* 'oh! he'='him' (Wright, *Arab. Gramm.* 103–104; cp. 294–295).

[4] Cp. Aram. *hăwāh* or *hăwâ*=Hebr. *hāyāh* 'became.'

[5] The position of the same ending now at the end and now at the beginning of the form to which it is attached is illustrated by the deictic -(*h*)*ā*- used in Hebrew and Aramaic as a mark of determination; for the Hebr. *ha-* at the beginning can hardly be dissociated from the Aram. *-â* at the end of determined nouns.

[6] Sayce (in *J.R.A.S.*, N.S. IX. 50–52) is therefore probably right in suggesting that this *t* is connected with the Egyptian feminine article (cp. Eg. *pꜣ nṯr* 'the god' with *tꜣ nṯr. t* 'the goddess'); it is probably connected also with the *t*- prefixed to certain abstract nouns (*e.g.* Acc. *tāḫazu^m* 'battle' and Hebr. *tagmûl* 'recompense'), especially as such nouns are in essence feminine, even though they may be treated as masculine for purposes of syntax.

[7] Gelb, *Inscriptions from Alishar and Vicinity*, 41–42.

VI

Vocalization of Verbal Forms

The choice of the final vowel in the various pseudo-verbal or verbal forms in the Semitic languages is a problem of considerable complexity, which must now be considered; for, in the first place, no entirely satisfactory solution of it has yet been propounded and, secondly, the explanation here offered, if it is accepted, affords additional proof that the structure of the Hebrew language is composite. This theory, of which something will be said below,[1] is the basis of the present attempt to account for the apparent vagaries of the Hebrew verb.

Lambert[2] has suggested in an article having especial reference to the Arabic verb that the characteristic vowel both of the perfect and of the imperfect tenses is determined not by the active or stative significance of the verb but by the nature of the consonant or consonants adjoining it. The following is a summary of his theory. That the vowels *a* and *i* or *u* are not marks respectively of active and stative verbs is proved by the fact that each is often found where the sense requires one of the others: thus the active *a* is found in the Hebrew stative imperfect *yik̲bad̲* 'is heavy,' and the stative *i* is found in the Arabic active perfect *qabila* 'received.' Since, then, the vocalization does not depend on the meaning of the verb, it must be in some way connected with the consonants composing the root. Now the consonants of the Arabic alphabet may be divided into three main classes, of which each prefers one or other of the three vowels, according to the following scheme: surds, consisting of labials (*w*, *b*, *f*, *m*) and emphatics (*ṣ*, *ḍ*, *q*, *j*, *š*) and hard gutturals (*h*, *ḥ*), which prefer *u*; what he calls *grêles*, consisting of liquids (*m*, *l*, *n*, *r*[3]) and sibilants (*t̲*, *d̲*, *ẓ*, *z*, *s*) and soft gutturals (' and ʿ), which prefer *i*; and what he calls *claires* (*t*, *d*, *ṭ*, *ẖ*, *k*, *ǧ*), which take indifferently *a* or *i* or *u*. Lambert also assumes that *a* must have been the primitive vowel both of the perfect and of the imperfect tenses, because it is the first vowel uttered by infants. Roots, however, which had a *grêle* as the second and especially as the third radical changed the second *a* into *i*, whereby *qatila* was produced; others with a surd as the second or third radical took *u*, whereby *qatula* was produced. Examples may be seen of the first

[1] S. pp. 98–107. [2] In *J.As.* VIII. xv. 169–174.

[3] Lambert writes *y*, but this must be an error for *r* as the argument shows.

process in *qabila* 'met' 'received' and *ḥazina* 'was sorry' and of the second in *ḥaṣuna* 'was strong' and *qabuḥa* 'was ugly.' Since, however, the principal verbs ending in a liquid were those expressing mental or spiritual states, it was natural that *i* should come to be regarded as proper to such verbs, and so, for example, *ġaḍiba* 'was angry' took *i* by analogy, although neither of its last two radicals belonged to the *i*-class of consonants. In the same way, as the principal verbs ending in surds expressed physical qualities, they naturally took *u*, and so again by analogy *hasuna* 'was beautiful' took *u*, although neither of its last two radicals belongs to the *u*-class of consonants. Thus a system of vocalization originally purely phonetic became semantic, even though analogy did not entirely override the phonetic principle: for example, *ʿamila* 'worked' retained the *i* which it owed to the phonetic principle without changing it into *a* (as it might be expected to have done on the analogy of the majority of active verbs, just as *faʿala* 'did' retained its primitive *a* without changing it into the *i* required by the same principle, although indeed Lambert does not go so far as to say this). It will have become clear that in the perfect tense only the second and third radicals come into force; in the imperfect tense, however, the first radical is brought into play, since by the ellipse of the immediately following vowel it is brought into approximate contact with the vowel between the second and third radicals (*e.g.* in *ya-qtalu* as contrasted with *qa-tala*). Since then in the Semitic languages surds predominated at the beginning, while *grêles* prevailed at the end, of triliteral roots, on the one hand *u* naturally tended to replace *a*; on the other hand the influence of *grêles* made itself felt in the imperfect of those verbs in which it had not been felt in the perfect tense both because the *a* of the first radical in the perfect did not exist in the imperfect form and also because *u* is more alien than *a* to the nature of *grêles*. Thus *ḍaraba* 'struck' preserved *a* in spite of the liquid *r*, which however exercised a kind of compensatory influence as the cause of the *i* in *yaḍribu* 'strikes' in spite of the presence of the two surds *ḍ* and *b*. This theory, at any rate as its author sets it out, is obviously unsatisfactory. First, the reason for assuming that *a* was the original vowel in both tenses recalls the proof whereby Psammetichus, as Herodotus [1] recounts, established the priority in time of Phrygian over all the other languages of mankind; and indeed the rarity of *qaṭal* and *iqṭal* in Accadian, which in most respects seems to have preserved the oldest forms of the Semitic verb, is against such a supposition. Second, it is

[1] In *Hist.* ii. 2.

At this point it is worth notice that a few Accadian permansive forms, generally besides having the regular form with *a* in the first and *i* in the second syllable, occasionally substitute *u* for *a* in the first or for *i* in the second syllable: such are of the former class *qurib* 'was near'; of the latter class *epuš* 'was made,' *gamur* 'was complete,' *daḫud* 'was abundant,' *limun* 'was evil,' *maqut* 'fell,' *maruṣ* 'was ill,' *raḫuṣ* 'was trusted,'[1] *šapuḫ* 'was spread out,' *ṣaruḫ* 'was mighty,' to which must be added two (*namur*, *ṣaduq*) from Tall-al-ʿAmârna. There is only one factor common to these otherwise very diverse verbs, namely that all except one contain the guttural *ḫ* or the palato-guttural *q* or the labials *m* and *p*. Zimmern,[2] therefore, seems to have been right in suspecting, and subsequent inquiry will confirm the suspicion, that *u* is preferred by the labial *b*/*p* and *m* whenever possible, and it must also be admitted that their influence may be either progressive or regressive; the *ō* in the Hebr. *qāṭōl* will be seen to be due to the same cause.[3] The only exception is *maruṣ*,[4] where the emphatic *ṣ* may be responsible for the displacement of *i* by *u*, as it seems to be also elsewhere.[5]

In Palestine the primitive permansive state has for the reasons hereafter given[6] become a perfect tense with an exclusively active significance; here then the stative-passive *i* has given place to the active *a*, and the truly verbal *qatal* 'he has killed' comes into existence beside the properly nominal *qatil*. This tendency is already apparent in the language of the letters from Tall-al-ʿAmârna[7] but is fully developed only in Biblical Hebrew; and here Ungnad[8] is probably right in suggesting that the process has been hastened or facilitated by the Hebrew rule that *i* in a closed accented syllable becomes *a* and also by the analogy of verbs with a hard guttural as medial or final consonant. At the same time *qāṭēl* remains the norm for most stative and a few intransitive verbs as set out in the following list:

(a) purely stative:

gāḇēr[9] 'was strong'	*ḥāmēṣ* 'was sour'	*kāšēr* 'was proper'
gāḏēl[9] 'was great'	*ṭāhēr* 'was pure'	*nāʿēm* 'was pleasant'
dāšēn 'was fat'	*ṭāmēʾ* 'was unclean'	*ʿāṣēm*[9] 'was mighty'
zāqēn 'was old'	*yāḇēš* 'was dry'	*šāpēl* 'was low'
	kāḇēḏ 'was heavy'	

---

[1] Possibly artificially dissimilated from *raḫiṣ* and *riḫiṣ* (Knudtzon, *A.-T.* 127. 33) 'was flooded, was overwhelmed.'

[2] In *Z.A.* V. 397–398 (s. pp. 55–56).

[3] S. pp. 52–53.

[4] Also *mariṣ*, where the *i* is preserved with the aid of the sonant *r* (s. pp. 55–56).

[5] S. pp. 64, 65; cp. Brockelmann, *G.V.G.S.S.* I. § 74 d β (in Arabic), i ε (in Hebrew).

[6] S. pp. 81–83.

[7] Cp. Böhl, *Spr. d. Amarnabr.* 43–45.

[8] In *B.A.S.S.* V. 247–248.

[9] Perfect tense, both *qāṭēl* and *qāṭal*.

(b) active but properly intransitive :

'āhēḇ [1,2] 'loved'		*qāmēl* [1] 'mouldered'
'āpēs 'came to an end'	*ḥāpēr* 'was ashamed'	*qārēḇ* [1] 'came near'
'āšēm [1] 'trespassed'	*yāʿēp* 'grew weary'	*rāʿēḇ* 'hungered'
bāsēq 'swelled'	*yārē'* 'feared'	*śāḇēaʿ* [1] 'was sated'
dāḇēq [1] 'clung'	*lāḇēš* [1,2] 'was clothed'	*śāmēaḥ* [1] 'rejoiced'
ḥāḏēl 'ceased'	*nāḇēl* [1,2] 'faded'	*śānē'* [2] 'hated'
ḥānēp [1] 'was polluted'	*ʿāšēš* 'was diseased' [3]	*šāḵēn* [1,2] 'dwelt'
ḥāsēr [1] 'lacked'	*ṣāmē'* 'thirsted'	*šāmēm* [2] 'was desolated'
ḥāpēs 'was delighted'	*qāḏēš* 'was hallowed'	*šāmēaʿ* [1,2] 'heard'

Some of these verbs have forms not only with *ē* but also with *a* existing side by side, just as the Bab. *nakar* 'he is hostile' [4] occurs beside *nakirat* 'she is hostile' [5] in the tablets from Tall-al-ʿAmârna ; some, too, take not *qāṭēl* but *qōṭēl* as the type of their participles. Only three of the purely stative verbs have forms both with *ē* and with *a*, and it is interesting that two of these (*gāḇēr*, *'āšēm*) come near to denoting an activity.[6] It is also noticeable that the only two apparently stative verbs which have *a* instead of *ē* are *ḥāḵam* 'was wise' and *qāṣar* 'was short' ; but the first seems originally to have meant 'understood' or the like, as the Acc. *ḫakāmu* 'to understand' used (like *lamāḏu* 'to learn') with the accusative case [7] shows, and the second means rather 'fell short,' so that both are really not stative in the strict sense but denote forms of activity. The M. Hebr. *qāṣēr* 'was short' and the Arab. *ḥakuma* 'was wise' represent the developments of artificial dissimilation common in the Semitic languages of the post-Christian period. Of the active verbs all describe conditions coming very near to passive states ; even the three which are normally construed as transitive verbs (*'āhēḇ*, *yārē'*, *śānē'*) really describe emotions and are therefore intransitive verbs limited in their application by nouns in the accusative case.[8] This point at once becomes clear if all the verbs assimilated to *qāṭal* are carefully considered when grouped together in the following list :

'āḇaḏ [9] 'perished'	*mālaḵ* 'became king'	*rāḇaṣ* 'crouched'
'āḇal 'mourned'	*māʿal* 'acted faithlessly'	*rāḡaz* 'quivered'
'āmar 'spoke'	*māraḏ* 'rebelled'	*rāḵaḇ* 'rode'
hālaḵ 'went'	*māšal* 'ruled'	*rāmaś* 'crept'
ḥāzaq 'prevailed'	*nāpal* 'fell'	*šāḇaṯ* 'desisted'
ḥālam 'dreamt'	*nāšaḵ* 'kissed'	*šāḵaḇ* 'lay down'
ḥālap 'passed on'	*nāṭaḵ* 'flowed forth'	*šālaṭ* 'domineered'
ḥāmal 'had compassion'	*ʿāḇar* 'crossed over'	*šāqaḏ* 'was wakeful'
ḥāraḏ 'trembled'	*ʿālaz/s/ṣ* 'exulted	*šāqaṭ* 'was peaceful'
yāṣaṯ 'kindled'	*ʿāmaḏ* 'stood'	*šāraṣ* 'swarmed'
kāšal 'stumbled'	*ʿāmal* 'toiled'	*šāraq* 'hissed'
	qāṣap 'was angry'	

---

[1] Perfect tense, both *qāṭēl* and *qāṭal*.
[2] Participle *qōṭēl*.
[3] In Ps. *31.* 11 (cp. Arab. *ġaṯṯa* 'was purulent, rotten'; s. Lambert in *R.É.J.* XXXIX. 302–303).
[4] Knudtzon, *A.-T. 298.* 23.
[5] *Ibid. 335.* 16.
[6] Cp. *ḥāzaq* 'grew strong, prevailed.'
[7] Rawlinson, *C.I.W.A.* IV.^{2} 60* C Obv. 16–17.
[8] S. p. 66.
[9] S. p. 12.

As in the second of the preceding lists, all these verbs are intransitive but describe not passive states but states of activity or acts. It is easy to see how the Accadian permansive (passive) *abit* 'was destroyed' and *emid* 'was put'[1] became respectively the Hebrew active (but intransitive) *'āḇaḏ* 'perished' and *'āmaḏ* 'stood'; and the contrast between the passive activity of *šāmēᵃ'* 'heard' and the creative activity of *'āmar* 'spoke' makes the difference between these two classes of active but at bottom intransitive perfectly clear. Now in the *ē*-class 27 out of 39 verbs and in the *a*-class 26 out of 34 verbs contain a liquid and/or a sibilant letter, which are known to have a preference for the *i*-vowel;[2] but the proportion of such roots in these two classes is so close that this fact cannot have been a determining factor in the maintenance of the *ē* in the Hebrew *qāṭēl* any more than it is responsible for the *i* in the Accadian *qaṭil*. In both cases, then, the vowel must have a semantic origin, *i.e.* it must be connected with the meaning. If this is so, the rule seems to be that *i* > *ē* has been preserved in those verbs which approximate most closely in meaning to the permansive state, *i.e.* which are purely stative, but that when the meaning is clearly active it gives place to *a*; between these two classes, which are of course bounded by no hard lines, are a number of verbs semantically ambiguous which incline now to the one and now to the other side. In these the *ē*-forms, which are frequently used only in pause, are reversions to the primitive type of the permansive *qatil*,[3] while the *a*-forms represent the tendency of the Western languages to assimilate all except purely stative verbs to the norm of the properly transitive *qatal*. Here, then, there are two distinct principles at work, the one (proto-Semitic) Eastern with its exclusive preference for *qatil* even in an active or transitive sense, the other Western with its retention of this form for stative verbs and its increasing tendency towards *qatal* for all active verbs.

Joüon,[4] after comparing a number of verbs in the various Semitic languages, reaches conclusions more or less in harmony

[1] The Acc. *abātu* 'to destroy' and *emēdu* 'to put' are both transitive verbs.

[2] S. pp. 55–56.

[3] Other pausal forms often represent other elements in the language: for example, the Hebr. *šāḵēn* in pause preserves the old (Eastern) permansive *i* seen in the Acc. *šakin* 'was put' (cp. Syr. *šken* 'was settled') and *šāḵan* out of pause has acquired the new (Western) perfect *a* seen in the Arab. *sakana* 'was still, stopped'; so too in pause the Hebr. *giddal* corresponding with the Arab. *qáttala* and the Eth. *qattála* makes *giddēl* and the Hebr. *hiṯqaddᵉšû* makes *hiṯqaddāšû* behind which lie respectively the Aram. *qaṭṭil* and *hiṯqaṭṭal*, and the Hebr. *yērēḏ* makes *yēraḏ* behind which lie forms respectively like the Acc. *ēṣir* (cp. Arab. *yaisiru*) and the Aram. *yêraṯ* (cp. Eth. *yeras*). In fact, many pausal forms in Hebrew will be found to reflect the proto-Semitic languages or the various Semitic dialects which have gone to the composition of the classical language.

[4] In *M.U.–St. J.* XV. 13–28.

with the views here expressed. He holds that the stative *qatil(a)* may become *qatal(a)* for three reasons: these are the influence of the consonants on the medial vowel, the ready transition of a stative into an active sense, and the analogy of the naturally enormous preponderance of active verbs. If then *qatil(a)* is found in any given root in any of the languages or even in a single dialect, that and not *qatal(a)* is likely to be the true form of the root. For example, the Eth. *re'eya* against the Hebr. *rā'āh* and the Arab. *ra'ay* 'saw' is in favour of an original *qatil(a)*, and this view is supported by the fact that verbs denoting perception are often of that form; that it has become *qatal(a)* in two languages will have been due to the analogy of the vast majority of active and transitive verbs.

He then tabulates a number of verbs which take *qatil(a)* in all or several of the Semitic languages and shows that they fall into eleven classes according to their meanings (illustrating them at the same time by a comparison of various Latin verbs of similar meaning which belong to the original stative second declension). The categories, together with his examples (with a few modifications), are arranged according to the meanings which they bear in the following list:

(i) states and qualities:[1]

Hebr. *zāqēn* 'was old'
Syr. *smeq* 'was red'
pleg 'was half'
Arab. *ẖaḏira* 'was green'
Aram. *n^epēš* 'was much'
šḥen 'was hot'
šmen 'was fat'

(ii) conditions analogous to states and qualities:[2]

Hebr. *yāšēn* 'slept'
Syr. *dmeḵ* 'slept'
Arab. *'alifa* 'was wont'
qaniʻa 'was content'
taʻiba 'was tired'
labisa 'wore'
sahira 'slept'
yaqiẓa 'was awake, cautious'

(iii) positions, situations, attitudes:[3]

Syr. *yīṯeḇ* 'sat'
rkeḇ 'rode'
sgeḏ 'bowed down'
škeḇ 'lay down'
Arab. *dabiqa* 'clung'
lazima 'applied oneself'
lasiqa 'adhered'

(iv) states of the body and sensations:[4]

Hebr. *ṣāmē'* 'was thirsty'
rāʻēḇ 'was hungry'
Syr. *kpen* 'hungered'
Arab. *ʻaṭiša* 'thirsted'

(v) perceptions of the senses:[5]

Arab. *'aḏina* 'hearkened'
samiʻa 'heard'
baṣira 'saw'
ṭaʻima 'tasted'

of the mind:

Arab. *jahila* 'was ignorant'
faqiha 'comprehended'
ʻalima 'knew'
fahima 'understood'

[1] Cp. Lat. *senere*; *rubere*; *arere calere, fervere, torrere*; *tumere, turgere*; *virere*.
[2] Cp. Lat. *solere*; *languere*; *cavere*.
[3] Cp. Lat. *sedere, jacere*; *haerere*.
[4] Cp. Lat. *horrere*.
[5] Cp. Lat. *videre*.

showing a predilection for *u* [1] and in the second case to the transitive meaning which the root has come to have.

The transitive sense of the Accadian *qatil*, though rare, is well attested, as in *qātē ilūtišu rabīti ṣabit* 'the hands of his great divinity he seized.' [2] The Hebrew *qāṭēl* however is strictly transitive only in *ḥāṣēḇ* 'hewed out' and occasionally in *mālē'* 'was full, filled.' The first occurs in a single passage [3] and is so entirely alien to Hebrew usage that it must be regarded as an error of vocalization. The second, however, has the support of the Acc. *mali* 'was full, filled' [4] and is so explicable; but there are traces of an alternative transitive *mālā'* 'filled' [5] (unless this vocalization comes from an acquaintance on the part of the Massoretes with the Arab. *mala'a* 'filled' as distinct from *mali'a* 'was full,' which is perhaps due to late and artificial differentiation), which may be the true form in this sense. A few other Hebrew verbs are generally cited in the dictionaries as having both transitive and intransitive meanings; this, however, is not really the case. Either they ought to be classified neither as transitive nor as intransitive but as active (such as *gāmar* 'came to an end,' *sāḵan* 'profited') or they are active but intransitive verbs with which the accompanying noun in the accusative case is not the direct object but introduces a qualification of place (such as *'āḇar* 'passed') or product (such as *nāṭap* 'dripped') or else they are active and transitive verbs with the ellipse of some such natural object as 'self' or 'back' or 'side' (such as *gāmal* 'ripened,' *hāpaḵ* 'turned,' *ḥālaṣ* 'withdrew,' *sāmaḵ* 'leaned,' *šāṭap* 'overflowed'). Further, it must never be forgotten that these apparent confusions of transitive and intransitive forms in many cases depend solely on the Massoretic vocalization; thus it is possible that all the transitive forms at any rate of one verb (*'āraṣ* 'was awestruck, struck with awe') ought to be vocalized not as Qal, as in the Massoretic text, but as *Pi'ēl*, if not as *Hip'il*. [6]

Lastly, Hebrew has a few permansive-perfect forms vocalized *qāṭōl* like the Accadian *qaṭul*. To this class belong, according to the Palestinian tradition, *yāgōr* 'was afraid,' *yāḵōl* 'was able,' *yāqōš* 'laid a bait,' *qāṭōn* 'was small,' *šāḵōl* 'was bereaved'; and there must be added, according to the Babylonian tradition, *bāṭōḥ* 'trusted,' *kāḇōḏ* 'was heavy,' [7] *mālōḵ* 'ruled.' [8] Here it

[1] S. pp. 53, 55. [2] Lehmann, *Šamaššumukīn*, II. 26–27, L[4] iii. 6 (s. pp. 114–116).
[3] Is. *5*. 2.
[4] Cp. Aram. *mᵉlâ* 'was full, filled' (s. p. 24). The Acc. *mali* in the permansive state seems only rarely to have a transitive sense (*e.g.* Tallqvist, *Maql.* 34–35, i. 35).
[5] In *mᵉlā'ô* 'it has filled him' (Esth. *7*. 5; s. Joüon, *Gramm. de l'hébr. bibl.* § 78 j).
[6] S. pp. 65, 82.
[7] In the Bab. *kabutu* (Knudtzon, *A.–T. 129*. 16) the *u* is due to assimilation to the plural affix in view of the singular *kabit* (Knudtzon, *op. cit. 11*. Rev. 23; cp. *88*. 47).
[8] Bergsträsser, *Hebr. Gramm.* II. § 14 d.

will at once be seen that the meaning is not a satisfactory key to the vocalization. A comparison of *yārē'* with *yāḡōr* shows this, since it cannot be said that the one denotes a transitory and the other a permanent state; nor are these verbs all stative, as *yāqōš* and *mālōḵ* at any rate are clearly active verbs. The vocalization, then, must depend on something else than the meaning; and that the nature of the consonants is the underlying cause of it becomes clear when it is remarked that six out of eight of these verbs contain in the second and/or third place a labial *b* or the palato-guttural *k* or *q*, which have been seen to occur in the majority of the Accadian cases of the permansive *qaṭul*.[1] The only exceptions are *qāṭōn* and *bāṭōḥ*; in these, however, the *ō* may be explained as due to the emphatic *ṭ* which exhibits a similar preference elsewhere.[2] Further, in seven cases the effective consonant has progressive but in one it has regressive force; again, therefore, influence either way must be admitted. The outcome, then, of this discussion is that two or three influences are at work in the vocalization of the Western perfect tense, namely the meaning which the word has and the nature of the consonants adjoining the significant vowel as well as the analogy of other verbs.

The case of the Accadian present and preterite tenses is not so easy as that of the permansive state, but an examination of all the strong verbs[3] which Muss-Arnolt's *Concise Dictionary of the Assyrian Language* (1905) contains shows that there are three schemes of vocalization in regular use. These are *qaṭil—iqaṭal—iqṭul*, *qaṭil—iqaṭul—iqṭul*, *qaṭil—iqaṭil—iqṭil*; of these the first is far the commonest, then comes the third, and after that the second, as the following lists show:

I. Present *iqaṭal*, preterite *iqṭul*.[4]

Transitive verbs:

baqāmu 'to shear'	*madādu* 'to measure'	*sapānu* 'to overthrow'
batāqu 'to cut through'	*maḫāḫu* 'to pour out'	*sarāqu* 'to pour'
dagālu 'to see'	*matāḫu* 'to spread out'	*paḫāru* 'to assemble'
dalāḫu 'to disturb'	*nazāru* 'to curse'	*paṭāru* 'to set loose'
dalālu 'to serve'	*naṭālu* 'to behold'	*parāsu* 'to divide'

[1] S. p. 46.

[2] S. pp. 51–52, 55; cp. Brockelmann, *G.V.G.S.S.* I. § 74 d β (in Arabic), i ε (in Hebrew). It is also significant that the verbs with the perf. *qṭôl* in the Christian-Palestinian Aramaic dialect (namely, *dbôr* 'took away,' *ykôl* 'ate,' *spôq* 'poured out,' *'ṭôp* 'covered,' *šbôq* 'left,' *smô'* 'heard'), where the meaning is no guide to the vocalization (Schultess, *Gramm. d. chr.-pal. Aram.* § 137 a–b), have one or other of the consonants here found to prefer *u* or *ô* with few exceptions. The same thing is true of the Babylonian Aramaic dialect (s. Levias *Gr. of the Aram. Id., B.T.* § 236 c).

[3] Accadian grammar recognizes no distinct class of stative verbs (except in so far as the permansive *qatil* has or may have a stative force), geminate verbs are not weak, and the weakness of those with initial *n* does not effect the final vowel.

[4] Verbs of which the forms or meanings are open to doubt are omitted from the various lists.

zakāru 'to declare'	*nasāḫu* 'to tear out'	*pašāru* 'to release'
zanānu 'to adorn'	*nasāqu* 'to praise'	*pašāšu* 'to anoint'
ḫabātu 'to rob'	*napāḫu* 'to kindle'	*ṣarāpu* 'to dye'
ḫasāsu 'to have in mind'	*napāṣu* 'to shatter'	*qanāqu* 'to seal'
ḫašālu 'to crush'	*naṣāru* 'to preserve'	*qaṣāṣu* 'to cut up'
ṭarādu 'to drive away'	*naqāru* 'to destroy'	*šadādu* 'to drag'
kabāsu 'to tread down'	*našāru* 'to deduct'	*šaṭāru* 'to write'
kaṣāru 'to join'	*sabāsu* 'to turn aside'	*šalālu* 'to despoil'
kašādu 'to catch'	*saḫālu* 'to pierce'	*šarāpu* 'to burn'
katāmu 'to cover'	*saḫāpu* 'to destroy'	*tamāḫu* 'to hold'
lapātu 'to upset'	*salāḫu* 'to sprinkle'	*tarāku* 'to smash'
laqātu 'to gather'	*sapāḫu* 'to scatter'	*tarāṣu* 'to stretch out'

Intransitive verbs :

ḫamāṭu 'to flare up, to hasten'[1] *ṣarāḫu* 'to cry out.'

The numbers are 51 transitive to 2 intransitive verbs; clearly, then, this scheme is proper to transitive verbs. The reason too is clear so soon as the priority of the present over the preterite tense is admitted:[2] as the soft *i* was chosen as the characteristic vowel of the original stative or passive permansive state, so the hard *a* was chosen as the opposite, *i.e.* as that of the active or transitive present tense, which was the next form in order of development; the only remaining vowel was *u* which, as different from that of the permansive state and the present tense, was the only choice left for the last, *i.e.* the preterite tense. Why a few verbs with both transitive and intransitive meanings—such as *gamāru* 'to be finished, to finish,' *karābu* 'to incline graciously, to accept graciously,' *magāru* 'to be favourable, to regard favourably,' *maḫāru* 'to correspond, to confront,' *saḫāru* 'to be turned round, surround,' *radādu* 'to go after, to pursue'—belong to this class is not obvious; some may have been originally or may have most frequently served as transitive verbs, while others may have been influenced by the analogy of other transitive verbs. Why also *ḫamāṭu* and *ṣarāḫu*, which are solely intransitive in meaning, are here is difficult to say, but it may be tentatively suggested that they may originally have belonged to the following class and that the *a* in the present tense is due to vowel-harmony.[3]

II. Present *iqaṭul*, preterite *iqṭul*.

Transitive verbs :

marāqu 'to rub' *mašāḫu* 'to survey' *nasāku* 'to set up'

Intransitive verbs :

balāṭu 'to live'	*maqātu* 'to fall'[4]	*raqādu* 'to hop'
damāmu 'to sigh'	*napāšu* 'to breathe'	*šamāḫu* 'to flourish'
ḫalālu 'to play the flute'	*sarāru* 'to be refractory'	*šaqāmu* 'to roar'
ḫapāpu 'to stoop down'	*ṣarāru* 'to shine'	*šarāru* 'to gleam'
kanāšu 'to be submissive'	*ramāmu* 'to howl'	*tarāru* 'to quake'

[1] The pres. *yiḫamita* (Winckler in Schrader's *K.B.* V. *63.* Rev. 6) ought to be read *yuḫamita* (Knudtzon, *A.-T. 129.* 78).

[2] S. pp. 29–31. [3] S. p. 60.

[4] Only secondarily 'to befall' with an acc. case.

In this list 8 out of 15 of the intransitive verbs contain a labial *p* or *m* and/or a guttural *ḫ* or a palatal *k* or *q* in the second place in the root, while one contains an emphatic *ṭ*, which is known to prefer *u* elsewhere in the Semitic languages and here has regressive effect on the preceding vowel,[1] in the third place; but the percentage of these verbs is hardly high enough to suggest that this is the cause of the vocalization, and it may be suggested that the *u* has been chosen as the vowel most closely related to *i* and therefore as most appropriate to intransitive verbs, when it is desired to avoid *i* as already in use in the permansive state. That this is so is curiously confirmed by the fact that *zaqāpu* 'to arise, to erect' follows both this and the preceding scheme according to the sense; for *izaqap-izqup* is transitive and *izaqup-izqup* is intransitive in meaning. Lastly, it may be suggested that *marāqu* and *mašāḫu* and *nasāku* owe their presence in this class, in which *u* is the rule in both tenses, to the fact that they each have one of the consonants known to prefer that sound, *ḫ* or *k/q*, in the third place in the root and that through their influence the transitive *a* has been displaced by the intransitive *u* in the present tense.[2]

III. Present *iqaṭil*,[3] preterite *iqṭil*.

Transitive verbs:

bašāmu 'to make'	*nad/tānu* 'to give'	*pašāṭu* 'to efface'
gamālu 'to spare'	*nakāmu* 'to heap up'	*patāqu* 'to prepare'
zabālu 'to carry'	*nakāsu* 'to cut down'	*qabāru* 'to bury'
ṭapālu 'to besmear'	*našāqu* 'to kiss'	*raṣāpu* 'to join'
kasāru 'to dam off'	*sadāru* 'to arrange'	*šabāṭu* 'to beat'
labānu 'to make in a mould'	*sakāpu* 'to overwhelm'	*šabāru* 'to break'
mašādu 'to oppress'	*sakāru* 'to stop up'	*šagāšu* 'to destroy'
	paqādu 'to entrust'	

Intransitive verbs:

damāqu 'to be good'[4]	*nazāzu* 'to stand'	*rapāšu* 'to be wide'
ḫalāqu 'to disappear'	*naḫāsu* 'to recede'	*šadāḫu* 'to proceed'
kazābu 'to be rich'	*namāru* 'to shine'	*šaḫāṭu* 'to ascend'
kamāsu 'to bow down'	*salāmu* 'to be gracious'	*šalāmu* 'to be whole'

Mixed (transitive and intransitive) verbs:

baṭālu 'to cease, to stop'	*nakāpu* 'to butt'	*sanāqu* 'to intrude, to oppress'
malāku 'to take counsel, to advise'		*parāku* 'to be in the way, to close'

Here 22 verbs are transitive, 12 are intransitive, 5 are mixed, though probably originally active but intransitive, in meaning; consequently that can hardly be the determining factor in the vocalization. It is, however, significant that out of these 39 verbs 14 contain a liquid and/or a sibilant letter in the second and 16 in the third place of the root; and it is a well-known fact that these letters have a definite preference

[1] S. pp. 51–52, 53; cp. Brockelmann, *G.V.G.S.S.* I. § 74 d β, i ε.
[2] S. pp. 46, 52–53, 60, 63–64.
[3] The variant *iqiṭil* found in some periods and styles is due to the assimilation of the medial to the initial and final vowel (cp. Eg.–Arab. *yimsik* and *yuskut*).
[4] Knudtzon, *A.–T.* *64.* 10; *85.* 33.

for the *i*-sound.[1] The suggestion that the *i* in this class is normally due to the action of the neighbouring consonant or consonants is confirmed by the fact that the variant infinitive *qiṭī/ēlu* is found almost exclusively under the same conditions: such verbs are *limīnu* 'to be evil,' *niḫīsu* 'to recede,' *namēru* 'to shine,' *naṣīru* 'to keep,' *sadīru* 'to arrange,' *sikīru* 'to stop up,' *pitēqu* 'to make,' *sa/iḫīru* 'to be small,' *qibīru* 'to bury,' *qirību* 'to approach,' *šebīru* 'to break.'[2] These show the vowel affected sometimes by the preceding and sometimes by the following consonant; one verb (*qibīru*) shows the first assimilated to the second vowel, since neither of the first two consonants prefer the *i*-sound, and one verb (*pitēqu*) is exceptional. This verb however and *paqādu*, as well as a few others, suggest that the weak dentals *d* and *t* may have had a tendency to require the *i*-sound.[3] Exceptional too are a few of the verbs in the preceding list (*nakāmu, sakāpu, paqādu, patāqu*), but these may have belonged originally to the first or second class according as they are transitive (*nakāmu, sakāpu, paqādu, patāqu*) or intransitive (*šadāḫu, šaḫāṭu*) in meaning; if so, the unexpected *i* in the present and preterite tense must be due to some form of assimilation, which will be discussed below.[4]

Primarily all Accadian verbs fall into one or other of these three schemes; yet neither scheme, either that resting on the meaning or that resting on the sound, has been entirely carried through, and it is often difficult to see why the one rather than the other has been preferred in any given case. Thus there seems no reason why the transitive *dalālu* should follow *iqaṭal-iqṭul* and the intransitive *ḫalālu* should follow *iqaṭul-iqṭul* when in view of their liquid *l* they might be expected to follow *iqaṭil-iqṭil*; in other words, why is sometimes the meaning and sometimes the sound the effective cause of the vocalization? Again, it is easy to understand why certain consonants (*b, p, m, ḫ, g, k, q, ṭ, ṣ*; *l, n, r, z, s, š*) should have a dominant effect when the other consonant in the root is neutral, but it is not so easy to see why a liquid or sonant or sibilant in the second place should be dominant over a labial or palato-guttural in the third place or why the reverse should sometimes happen. The problem, however, of the relative values of sound and position in assimilation remains yet to be worked out in detail.[5] At the same time very many variations from these

[1] Meissner, *K.A.G.* § 20 d.

[2] Also *parīsu, sakīpu, zaqīpu, nadīnu* (Bauer, *Inschriftenw. Assurb.* II. 1 on i. 20.)

[3] S. p. 72.

[4] S. pp. 58–62. This may often be the case with *n*-verbs in the preterite tense, where the final vowel comes into proximity to that of the prefix (s. pp. 58–59).

[5] The Sem. *šm* 'name,' becoming Acc. *šumu* and Aram. *šûmâ* but Hebr. *šēm* and Eth. *sem*, offers a good example of arbitrary assimilation; for there seems to be no reason why it is sometimes regressive and sometimes progressive.

three schemes can be explained as secondary developments due either to the effect of an adjoining consonant or to the influence of a neighbouring vowel resulting in the assimilation of the one to the other [1]; a few, too, may be due to the artificial dissimilation of roots whose forms are identical but whose meanings are distinct.[2] Lastly, the failure to account for the vagaries of any verbs on these grounds is probably due to the insufficient number of examples so far discovered.

First, an *a* or an *i* may become *u* under the influence of a labial *b*/*m*/*p* or a guttural *ḫ* or a palatial *g*/*k*/*q*, and an *a* or an *u* may become *i* under the influence of a liquid *l*/*n*/*r* or a sibilant *z*/*s*/*ṣ*/*š*, whether the consonant precedes or follows the vowel:

I-type (*iqaṭal-iqṭul*) with *a*>*u* in the present tense under labial or guttural influence:

ramāku 'to pour out'	*iramak* *iramuk*	*irmuk*
šaḫāṭu 'to strip'	*išaḫaṭ* *išaḫuṭ*	*išḫuṭ*

or with *a*>*i* in the present and/or *u*>*i* in the preterite tense under liquid or sibilant influence:

ḫašāḫu 'to desire'	*iḫašaḫ*	*iḫšuḫ* *iḫšiḫ*
karāru 'to put down'	*ikarar* [3]	*ikrur* *ikrir*
paqāru 'to demand'	*ipaqar* *ipaqir*	*ipqur* *ipqir*
raḫāṣu 'to inundate'	*iraḫaṣ*	*irḫuṣ* *irḫiṣ*
šarāku 'to give'	*išarak*	*išruk* *išrik*

II-type (*iqaṭul-iqṭul*) with *u*>*i* in either tense under liquid or sibilant influence:

qarābu 'to be near'	*iqarub* *iqarib*	*iqrub* *iqrib*
raḫāṣu 'to wait'	*iraḫuṣ*	*irḫuṣ* *irḫiṣ*

III-type (*iqaṭil-iqṭil*) with *i*>*u* in either tense under labial influence:

kapādu 'to devise'	*ikapid* *ikapud*	*ikpid* *ikpud*
labāru 'to be old'	*ilabir*	*ilbir* *ilbur*

In the first group the sense in every case shows to which class the verb must originally have belonged; all must have

[1] Ungnad (in *Z.D.M.G.* LIX. 767) is thus clearly right in suggesting that the *i* in *limad* is due to the liquid *l*, and this may be true also of *pilaḫ*; so the first *u* in *rukub* has been attracted to the second *u*, and that is due to the overwhelming effect of the palatal *k* and the labial *b*.

[2] S. pp. 46, 61, 67.

[3] S. p. 58.

been originally of the I-type (*qaṭil-iqaṭal-iqṭul*), as they have a transitive meaning; consequently the variant present *iqaṭul* in the first and the variant preterite *iqṭil* in the second divisions of this group must be due to the nature of one or other or of both the consonants accompanying the final vowel. Whether, however, *paqāru* may have belonged originally to the I-type or to the III-type cannot be decided; that depends on the answer to the question whether the meaning or the nature of the consonants is considered originally to have been the predominant influence in determining the vocalization. In the second and third groups the meanings are ambiguous, being now transitive and now intransitive; it is therefore evident that the factor determining the vocalization is in each case the consonant whether preceding or following the final vowel.

Second, a vowel may be assimilated to an immediately preceding or following vowel. In this way the vowel proper to the tense may be attracted to that of the pronominal prefix or affix: for example—

(i) to the *a*- of the singular first or the *i*- of third person:

nadānu 'to give'	*inadin* *anadan*	*iddin* *addan* [1]	(III)

(ii) to the -*ū* of the plural third person:

karāru 'to put down'	*ikarar* *ikaruru* [2]	*ikrur*	(I)
rakāsu 'to bind'	*irakas* *irakusu*	*irkus*	(I)
šaqālu 'to weigh'	*išaqal* *išaqulu*	*išqul*	(I)
tabāku 'to heap up'	*itabak* *itabuku*	*itbuk*	(I)

In each case it is clear to which class the verb belongs, and the alternative forms can be ruled out as due to causes extraneous to the formation of the tense itself.

Frequently the medial *a* of the present tense attracts the final vowel of the root to itself, as in the following forms arranged according to the class to which they belong:

II-type (*iqaṭul-iqṭul*) with final *u* assimilated to medial *a*:

dabābu 'to speak'	*idabub* *idabab*	*idbub*
zanānu 'to rain'	*izanun* *izanan*	*iznun*
ragāmu 'to roar'	*iragum* *iragam*	*irgum*
šaḫāḫu 'to bow down'	*išaḫuḫ* *išaḫaḫ*	*išḫuḫ*

[1] Usually *addin*; cp. *alsam* and *atkal* (s. pp. 59, 61). [2] S. p. 57.

III-type (*iqaṭil-iqṭil*) with final *i* assimilated to medial *a*:

nakāru 'to be strange'	*inakir*	*ikkir*
	inakar	
rabāṣu 'to crouch'	*irabiṣ*	*irbiṣ*
	irabaṣ	

The class to which the first four verbs properly belong is shown by the fact that they are intransitive in meaning, that of the last two is shown by the presence respectively of *ṣ* and *r* in the last place in the root.

Now two of these verbs (*paqāru*, *qarābu*) have the two types of inflexion, that dependent on the meaning and that dependent on the consonants, fully developed, and this suggests that many more, if not all of them, may have had double sets of tense-formations but that examples of all their forms have not yet been found. It is then permissible to assume that when a verb exhibits an incongruous combination of tenses, *i.e.* a present of one class and a preterite of another class, the proper preterite and present tenses respectively have fallen into disuse or have not yet been found in any known texts but may *a priori* be expected to occur. A number of verbs with such incongruous tenses are given in the following lists, in which is added in the margin the number of the class to which each probably belongs and the cause of the vocalization of the variant form:

lamānu 'to be evil'	*ilamin*		(III, owing to *n*).
	ilaman		(*i* assimilated to *a*).
		ilmun	(*i*>*u* after *m*).
lasāmu 'to run'		*ilsum* [1]	(II, intransitive).
	ilasam		(*u* assimilated to *a*).
mašālu 'to be like'		*imšil*	(III, owing to *š* and *l*).
	imašal		(*i* assimilated to *a*).
šalāpu 'to draw out'		*išlup*	(I, transitive).
	išalup [2]		(*a*>*u* before *p*)

Occasionally the class to which a verb belongs is uncertain. Thus *nabāṭu* 'to shine' makes *inabuṭ* but *ibbiṭ*: if it belongs to the *i*-class (which contains a few verbs without liquid or sibilant consonants), the *u* in the present tense is due to the labial *b*; but probably it belongs to the intransitive *u*-class, so that the *i* in the preterite tense is due to the progressive effect of the *i*-prefix. On the contrary, dissimilation occasionally comes into force. Thus *danānu* 'to be strong' has the imperfect *idanin* but the precative *ludnin* in the first person and *lidnun* in the third person; the double *n* suggests that it belongs to the *i*-class, so that *ludnin* preserves the correct *i* of the preterite tense while the *u* in *lidnun* will be due to artificial dissimilation.

[1] But *alsam*; cp. *addan* and *atkal* (s. pp. 58, 61).

[2] But *ašalap*, which in this case probably preserves the true form of the present tense.

If, then, it is accepted that most if not all of these verbs must or at any rate may have had two classes of inflexion fully developed side by side, the supposed irregular verbs will disappear; there will be no intransitive verbs with *iqaṭal-iqṭul* and no transitive verbs with *iqaṭil-iqṭil*. The following will then be the true paradigms:

(i) of the intransitive verbs apparently belonging to the former class:

ḫamāṭu 'to flare up,' 'to hasten'		*iḫmuṭ*	(II, intransitive)
	iḫamaṭ		(*u* assimilated to *a*)
ṣarāḫu 'to cry out'		*iṣruḫ*	(II, intransitive)
	iṣaraḫ		(*u* assimilated to *a*)

(ii) of the transitive verbs apparently belonging to the latter class:

marāqu 'to rub'		*imruq*	(I, transitive)
	imaruq		(*a*>*u* before *q*)
mašāḫu 'to survey'		*imšuḫ*	(I, transitive)
	imašuḫ		(*a*>*u* before *ḫ*)
nasāku 'to set up'		*issuk*	(I, transitive)
	inasuk		(*a*>*u* before *k*)

In each case the meaning shows to which class these verbs must be assigned, and the nature of one or other of the last two consonants is such as to account for the apparent irregularity in their vocalization.

Finally, Philippi[1] has explained the *a* in the preterite *iṣbat* (beside the expected *iṣbut*) as attracted to the final vowel in the present *iṣabat*, and this view seems to be right, as no other way of accounting for this *a* offers itself. Accordingly, the alternative form of the preterite may be explained as due to attraction to the present tense in the following verbs:

maḫāṣu 'to strike'	*imaḫaṣ*	*imḫuṣ*
		imḫaṣ
ṣabāru 'to snatch'	*iṣabar*	*iṣbur*
		iṣbar
ṣabātu 'to seize'	*iṣabat*	*iṣbut*
		iṣbat
šakānu 'to put'	*išakan*	*iškun*
		iškan
šapāru 'to send'	*išapar*	*išpur*
		išpar

All these verbs are transitive in meaning and therefore belong properly to the I-type (*iqaṭal-iqṭul*), so that it is not the *u* but the *a* of the preterite tense which is abnormal. There may also be classified with these verbs the following 6 quite peculiar verbs, which have only one form, that with *a*,

[1] In *B.A.S.S.* II. 385–387, where he needlessly extends the same principle to explain *islim* as attracted to *isalim* (s. pp. 55–56).

of the preterite tense, making present *iqaṭal* and preterite *iqṭal*:

lamādu 'to learn'	*palāḫu* 'to fear'[1]	*pašāḫu* 'to be soothed'[2]
ṣalālu 'to lie down'	*rakābu* 'to be mounted'[2]	*tabālu* 'to carry off'

Of these, 3 are transitive and 3 are intransitive verbs, so that the meaning can have nothing to do with the vocalization; nor can the consonants have exerted their influence on the neighbouring vowel, as they are mixed, some requiring *u* and others requiring *i*. It is then necessary to suppose that the final vowel in the present tense is due to the progressive influence of the medial *a* and that the vowel of the preterite has then been assimilated to that of the present tense. Thus the six difficult verbs (*nakāmu, sakāpu, paqādu, patāqu, šadāḫu, šaḫāṭu*) in the third group which unexpectedly follow the model of *iqaṭil-iqṭil*[3] may be similarly explained; the vowel of the present is due to assimilation to that of the preterite tense, of which the final vowel has been in its turn assimilated to that of the prefix. There remain the two following verbs:

marāṣu 'to be steep'	*imaraṣ*	*imruṣ* *imraṣ*
takālu 'to trust'	*itakil*	*itkal*

The first is an intransitive verb which ought to follow *iqaṭul-iqṭul* but in which the final *u* has been assimilated to the medial *a* in the present tense and the resulting *imaraṣ* has carried the preterite with it, although the regular *u* has maintained itself beside the exceptional *a* in that form. The second ought, in view of the final *l*, to follow *iqaṭil-iqṭil* as it does in the present tense, but the preterite *itkal* is hard to explain; perhaps it is due to attraction either to a lost present form with *a* in the final syllable assimilated to the medial *a* or to the first person, which beside the expected *atkil* has also *atkal* by obvious vowel-harmony.[4]

This principle, that one form can affect another form in its vocalization is not so strange as it may at first sight seem; for there are numerous instances of it in the other Semitic languages. For example, it becomes possible to invoke it in explanation of the *ē* (for the expected *a*) in the Hebr. *qiṭṭēl*[5] as due to the analogy of *y*^{e}*qaṭṭēl*[6] and the *î* in *hiqṭîl* (for the expected *a* > *i* > *ē*) to the analogy of *yaqṭîl* and that in *yaqṭîl*

[1] The *a* can hardly be due to the common Semitic attraction of *i* and *u* to that vowel under the influence of the following *ḫ* (cp. Brockelmann, *G.V.G.S.S.* I. § 74, a *a*), as that form of attraction is rare in Accadian grammar (cp. Meissner, *K.A.G.* § 20 a), and this will not in any case explain the other verbs in this list.

[2] But *irkub* 'he trembled' (Knudtzon, *A.-T. 56.* 34, cp. *147.* 14); cp. Hebr. *yirkab* (s. p. 71).

[3] S. pp. 55–56.

[4] Cp. *addan* and *alsam* (s. pp. 58, 59).

[5] Cp. Arab. *qáttala*, Eth. *qattála*.

[6] Cp. Kautzsch & Cowley, *Hebr. Gramm.* 140[1].

in its turn to the analogy of *yāqîm* [1] and similarly the *a* (for the expected *i*) in the Arab. *yataqattalu* [2] as due to the analogy of *taqattala*, and so on.

The verbs in the correspondence found at Tall-al-ʿAmârna are vocalized in the same way as ordinary Babylonian verbs, although a few variations from the forms already tabulated may here be set on record (with their Eastern vocalization following the Western form in brackets):

dabābu 'to speak'	*idabub* *idabib*	*idbub*	(*u–u*)
ḫalāqu 'to be lost'	*iḫalliq*	*iḫliq* *iḫlaq*	(*i–i*)
malāku 'to advise'	*imalik*	*imlik* *imluk*	(*i–i*)
naṣāru 'to preserve'	*inaṣar* *inaṣir* *inaṣur*	*iṣṣur*	(*a–u*)
nazāzu 'to stand'	*izzaz*	*izziz*	(*i–i*)
paṭāru 'to loosen'	*ipaṭar* *ipaṭir*	*ipṭur*	(*a–u*)
palāḫu 'to fear'	*ipalaḫ* *ipaliḫ*	*ipliḫ*	(*a–a*)
tarāṣu 'to stretch out'	*itaraṣ*	*itruṣ* *itriṣ*	(*a–u*)

The variations in this list are easily explained. The *i* in *ipaliḫ-ipliḫ* is due to the *l*, in *ipaṭir* and *itriṣ* it is due to the *r* (or the *r* and *ṣ* together, as the case may be); the *i* or *u* in *inaṣir* or *inaṣur* is produced by assimilation or partial assimilation to the same two letters; the *u* in *imluk* is caused by the influence of the *k* having prevailed over that of the *l*. In *iḫlaq*, which has *a* only in *aḫlaq* [3] and *teḫlaq*,[4] in the former case it is clearly due to assimilation to the *a* of the prefix,[5] in the latter it may be due to partial assimilation to the *e* of the prefix or perhaps rather to the analogy of the first person. In *idabib*, which occurs only once in *tidabbibu*,[6] the *i* may perhaps be explained as dissimilated from the *u* of the plural ending. Finally, the peculiar present *izzaz* (<*inaziz*) is probably due after the irregular contraction to artificial differentiation from the normal preterite *izziz* (<*inziz*). These forms, however, are of little interest except *imluk*, which shows a stage evidently transitional between the Accadian *imlik* [6] and the Hebrew *yimlōḵ*; [7] one principle has prevailed in the East, another in the West.

In some respects the problem of the Hebrew imperfect, owing to the absence of a present tense, is not so complex; yet it too is not free from difficulties. In Hebrew there are

[1] Cp. Kautzsch & Cowley, *Hebr. Gramm.* 144^{1}. [2] Cp. Hebr. *yiṯqaṭṭēl*.
[3] Knudtzon, *A.-T. 270.* 29; cp. *addan, alsam, atkal* (s. pp. 58, 59, 61).
[4] *Ibid. 274.* 14. [5] S. pp. 59–60, 62.
[6] Knudtzon, *A.-T. 138.* 49. [7] S. pp. 63–64.

again three schemes: these are, in order of frequency, *qāṭal-yiqṭōl* and *qāṭē/al-yiqṭal* and *qāṭal-yaqṭi/ēl*, as shown in the following tables.

I. Imperfect *yiqṭōl*.

To this class belong all transitive verbs except those containing a guttural as the second or third radical in the root; the choice of *u* > *ō* is due to the need of a vowel distinct from the *a* of the perfect tense and stronger than the passive or stative *i* > *ē*. Thus in vocalization though not in form the Acc. *iqaṭal* is to *iqṭul* as the Hebr. *qāṭal* is to *yiqṭōl*.[1] The bulk of the transitive verbs, therefore, in which the vocalization of the imperfect tense rests on the meaning, do not require to be tabulated. At the same time, the imperfect tense of a number of intransitive verbs is (incorrectly according to the meaning) *yiqṭōl*, and these are as given in the following table:

'ānaq 'groaned'
'āpaḏ 'wore the ephod'
'āraḇ 'lay in wait'
bāgaḏ 'acted treacherously'[2]
bāraq 'lightened'
dāgal 'raised a standard'
dālap 'dripped'
dāmam 'was silent'
hālaḵ 'went'[4]
ḥāgag 'went on pilgrimage'
ḥālam 'dreamed'
ḥālap 'passed on'
ḥāmal 'was sparing'
ḥāpaz 'was in trepidation'
ḥāpaṣ 'stooped'
ḥāpēṣ 'delighted'[6]
kāsap 'yearned'
kāšal 'stumbled'
māḵaḵ 'was low'
mālaḵ 'was king'[7]
mā'al 'dealt faithlessly'
māraḏ 'rebelled'
māšal 'ruled'
nāḇēl 'faded'
nāḏar 'vowed'
nāham 'growled'
nāpal 'fell'[3]
nāqam 'took vengeance'
nāqap 'went round'
nāšam 'panted'
sāḇaḇ 'went round'
sāgaḏ 'bowed down'
sāḵan 'profited'
sāpaḏ 'wailed'
'ābaṭ 'took a pledge'
'āṭap 'was enveloped; fainted; inclined'
'ālaz/s/ṣ 'exulted'
'āmaḏ 'stood'
'āmal 'toiled'
'āraḡ 'longed'
'ārap 'dripped'
qāsam 'divined'
qāṣap 'was wroth'
rāmaś 'crept'
rāqaq 'spat'
śāpaq 'sufficed'
šāḇaṯ 'ceased'
šāḥaḥ 'bowed down'
šāṭam 'grudged'
šāḵaḵ 'decreased'
šāḵē/an 'dwelt'[5]
šāqaḏ 'was watchful'
šāqaṭ 'was at rest'
šāqaq 'was emptied'
šāqar 'dealt falsely'
šāraṣ 'swarmed'
šāraq 'hissed'
šāṯaq 'was quiet'
šāmēm 'was desolate'
tāmam 'was complete'

Of these 63 verbs 3 or 4 are or may be vocalized as stative verbs with *ē*, and a few others with *a* in the perfect tense are also stative in meaning, while almost all the others are active but intransitive; all according to Hebrew rules ought, therefore,

[1] S. pp. 13, 93–94. The only Hebrew survivors of the primitive form with *u* < *û* are such nouns as *yaḥmûr* 'it is red' = 'roebuck' and *yalqûṭ* 'it collects' = 'wallet,' with the final vowel lengthened according to the Massoretic rule for the accentuation of nouns. Ungnad (in *B.A.S.S.* V. 253) is in favour of adding forms like the peculiar *yišpûṭû* (Ex. *18*. 26), but as these depend solely on the Massoretic vocalization, no evidential value or importance can be attached to them (Kautzsch & Cowley, *Hebr. Gramm.* § 47 g). Prätorius (in *Z.At.W.* III. 52–55) ascribes them to the analogy of *yāqûm*, but this does not account for their extreme rarity, which suggests mistaken tradition.

[2] The form and vocalization of *niḇgaḏ* (Mal. *2*. 10) are doubtful.

[3] Cp. Acc. *ippul* 'he felled.'

[4] Imperfect *yahălōḵ*; s. p. 69 for *yēlēḵ*.

[5] Cp. Acc. *iškun* 'he put.'

[6] The accusative case with this verb does not express the direct object.

[7] S. pp. 106–107.

to take *a* in the imperfect tense. On examination, however, the striking fact is revealed that 56 of these 63 verbs have a labial *b*/*p* or *m* or a guttural *ḥ* or a palatal *g*/*k*/*q* in the second or third place of the root, and these are the very letters which have been found in those Assyrian verbs which have been improperly vocalized with *u* in the present or preterite tenses. Even the 5 or 6 exceptions can be explained with little difficulty. In *mā'al* the ', which represents the velar *ǵ* as the Arab. *maǵala* 'slandered' shows, being akin to the guttural *ḫ*[1] is clearly responsible,[2] and in *'ālaṣ* (which is the true form of the root as the Acc. *elīṣu* 'to exult' shows) and in *šāraṣ* the *ṣ*[3] is properly responsible for the *u* of the imperfect tense. The same peculiarity is probably due in *māšal* to the analogy of *mālak* and in *mārad* to that of *bāgad* and *mā'al* as verbs of similar meaning; so, too, in *nādar* it may be due to the analogy of *nāzar* which is itself not found in the Qal but which seems to have been originally a transitive verb, as the cognate Acc. *nazāru* (pres. *inanzar*,[4] pret. *izzur*) 'to curse' suggests. Of *kāšal* there are only two instances of the imperfect tense of the Qal, and both of these are textually uncertain.[5]

There belong also to this class, in which *a* has been displaced by *ō* in the imperfect tense, six intransitive geminate verbs:

bālal 'gave provender'[6]	*'āzaz* 'was strong'	*qādad* 'bowed down'[7]
hālal 'boasted'	*pāzaz* 'was agile'	*rānan* 'rang out'

Here several causes may be at work, while in several cases it is impossible to say which, if not both, of the causes is responsible for the vocalization. Thus in 4 cases (*bālal*, *'āzaz*, *pāzaz*, *qādad*) the first consonant, coming immediately before the final vowel in the imperfect tense (*yibbōl* or *yābōl*, *yā'ōz*, *yāpōz*, *yiqqōd*) is clearly responsible for it;[8] in one or two (*rānan* and perhaps also *hālal*) the vowel may well be onomatopœic.[9] Again, in one or two cases (*'āzaz* and perhaps also *hālal*) the analogy of hollow verbs with medial *w* (Arab. *hāla* 'struck with awe,'[10] Hebr. *'ôz* 'to take refuge' and Arab. *'āḏa* 'sought

[1] O'Leary, *Comp. Gr. of the Sem. Lang.* 48–49.

[2] Cp. the K. *'eslôᵃḥ* for the Q. *'eslaḥ* (Jer. *5*. 7), apparently the sole case in the O.T. in which *ḥ*=*ḫ* (cp. Acc. *salāḫu* 'to besprinkle') retains its primitive preference for *u*/*ō* over its later tendency to take *a* (s. pp. 46, 52–53, 60).

[3] S. pp. 46, 65.

[4] For *inazzar*=*inázar*.

[5] Nah. *3*. 3; Prov. *4*. 16.

[6] Judg. *19*. 21, where the K. is *wayyibbôl*, while the Q. is *wayyābol*.

[7] Acc. *iqdud*.

[8] This principle is clearly operative also in the case of certain verbs whose first consonant is weak (s. p. 69).

[9] Thus *u* is clearly onomatopœic in a number of English words ('buzz,' 'burble,' 'gurgle,' 'rumble,' 'tumble'), and *u*/*ō* may have been to a certain extent so in several Accadian (*damāmu*, *ramāmu*, *šaqāmu*) and Hebrew (*hāmam*, *nāham*, *nāšam*; *'ānaq*) verbs; in this it is akin to the labial sound common to many such verbs.

[10] Lambert *ap.* Buhl, *Hebr. u. Aram. Hwb.* 183.

protection') may be the reason for the vocalization;[1] for geminate verbs are often incorrectly written *plene* with *ô* for *ō*, while many hollow *w*-verbs have *ō* instead of *û* in the imperfect tense.

That the theory here put forward is more or less correct is shown by the alternative forms of the imperfect tense of *ḥ̱ānan* 'inclined favourably';[2] for *yeḥĕnan* owes its *a* (unless it is a primitive *i* > *a*, due to the sonant *n*) to the originally intransitive meaning of the root, while *yāḥōn* owes its *ō* to the approximation of the initial guttural *ḥ* to the final vowel in this form of the tense.

To this class belong also the following verbs which have sometimes a transitive and sometimes an intransitive meaning:

gāmal 'weaned, ripened' 'became ripe'	*zāʿam* 'was enraged' 'denounced'	*sāmak̲* 'supported' 'leaned'
gāmar 'completed' 'came to an end'	*ḥālap* 'passed on' 'pierced'	*ʿāb̲ar* 'went by' 'crossed'
hāmam 'discomfited' 'made a disturbance'	*ḥālaṣ* 'drew off' 'withdrew oneself'	*ʿāraṣ* 'was awestruck' 'struck with awe'
hāpak̲ 'overturned' 'turned back'	*nāṭap* 'dripped' 'dropped'	*šāṭap* 'rinsed' 'overflowed'

Of these verbs it is evident that some are properly transitive verbs used intransitively through the ellipse of the natural object; in these the *ō* is the proper vowel of the imperfect tense. Others are equally clearly intransitive verbs of which the noun in the accusative is not the direct object but a pseudo-adverbial qualification; here the *ō* is due to the nature of the accompanying consonant, which in every case is one of those which have already been shown to have a preference for that vowel.[3] The only extreme case of a double meaning is *ʿāraṣ*; if this is properly intransitive, as the cognate Syriac and Arabic verbs suggest, the *ō* is due to the emphatic *ṣ*[4] so that its transitive form will be due to misvocalization.[5]

II. Imperfect *yiqṭal*.

To this class belong all stative verbs except three or four and the vast majority of active but intransitive verbs and most transitive verbs containing a guttural as their second or third consonant; these require no comment as they obey the well-known Hebrew rule that gutturals take *a* wherever possible.

[1] S. pp. 67–68.

[2] Clearly akin to *ḥ̱ānāh* 'declined' and so originally intransitive in meaning (cp. Jer. *22*. 23, where *nēḥantî* means 'thou didst bend thyself down' in the painful yearning of child-birth; s. Daiches in *P.E.F.Q.S. 59*. 163); s. pp. 67–68.

[3] It may therefore be doubted whether Buhl is right to alter *yigmōr* into *yigmar* when it has an intransitive meaning (Ps. 7. 10).

[4] S. pp. 46, 64.

[5] S. p. 52.

There are, however, a few transitive or apparently transitive vowels with *a* in the imperfect tense, as in the following list :

'āhēḇ 'loved'	*hāḏar* 'honoured'	*lāmaḏ* 'learned'
'āṭar 'shut up'	*ḥārap* 'taunted'	*qāram* 'spread over'
'ālap 'learned'	*ḥāraṣ* 'mutilated'	*rāpaḏ* 'spread out'

The first (*'āhēḇ*) is properly active but intransitive as expressing an emotion ;[1] two others (*'ālap*, *lāmaḏ*) too are probably in origin intransitive, and the noun in the accusative case with which they may be construed expresses not the direct object but that with or in which the subject is familiar or exercised.[2] Others (*ḥārap*, *ḥāraṣ*, *rāpaḏ*) are entered in the dictionaries as transitive as a result of mistranslation ; thus the meanings are respectively of *ḥārap* not 'taunted'[3] but 'was sharp, was cutting, *i.e.* was full of taunts'[4] (cp. Syr. *ḥarep* 'sharpened'), of *ḥāraṣ* not 'cut' or 'sharpened' but 'was sharp, was incisive'[5] or 'was decisive,'[6] of *rāpaḏ* not 'spread' but 'sprawled' (cp. Acc. *rapādu* 'to lie stretched out').[7] The remainder (*'āṭar*, *hāḏar*, *qāram*) are probably due to misvocalization. There is no reason why *'āṭar* should take *a*, unless *i* > *a* is due to the sonant *r*, and the fact that the cognate Arab. *'aṭara* 'bent over' takes the usual *u* in the imperfect tense suggests that *u*>*ō* is the proper vowel for this verb.[8] It is hardly possible that the Qal of *hāḏar* can be transitive ; the cognate Arab. *hadara* 'fermented' is intransitive and the Aram. *haddēr* (cp. Mishn. Hebr. *hiddēr*) 'adorned' suggests that the Hebrew verb ought similarly to be vocalized as Pi'ēl when used with a direct object.[9] Lastly, *qāram* is once transitive and once intransitive,[10] where however the Nip'al, which the Peshiṭtâ and Vulgate seem to imply, ought probably to be read.

In a few verbs it is not at first sight clear why they belong to this class, but a brief explanation will make it clear. These are :

nāšaḵ 'paid interest'	*nāšaq* 'kissed'
nāšal 'slipped off,' 'stripped off'	*pāṭar* 'set free,' 'departed'

---

[1] S. p. 47.

[2] Thus the accusative case is once displaced by a preposition (Jer. *10*. 2, where the object precedes the verb).

[3] The Pi. rather than the Q. means transitively 'taunted,' with a direct object in the accusative case.

[4] Jb. *27*. 6, where *yeḥĕraḇ lᵉḇāḇî* means 'my heart shall be cutting,' *i.e.* 'ready to utter taunts' ; the participle of the Q., however, is used with a pronominal suffix, but in a nominal sense, as often with other verbs.

[5] Ex. *11*. 7, where *yeḥĕraṣ keleḇ lᵉšōnô* means 'a dog shall be sharp as to his, *i.e.* shall show a sharp, tongue.'

[6] 2 Sam. *5*. 24, where *teḥĕrāṣ* means 'thou shalt be (*Angl.* look) sharp,' and 1 Ki. *20*. 40, where *ḥārāṣtā* means 'thou hast been sharp, *i.e.* hast acted in a decisive manner.'

[7] Jb. *41*. 22, where *yirpaḏ ḥārûṣ* means 'he sprawls (like) a threshing-board.'

[8] Ps. *69*. 16, where the Massoretes may have taken the verb in an intransitive sense, supposing *'al te'ṭar 'ālay bᵉ'er pīyāh* to mean, 'let not the pit be closed in respect to her mouth over me.'

[9] Ex. *23*. 3 ; Lev. *19*. 15, 32.

[10] Ezek. *37*. 8.

Probably the *a* in *yiššaḵ* was an artificial vocalization intended to distinguish it from *yiššōk* 'bit' with *ō*,[1] which is at bottom the same word, and the change was helped by the fact that, while *yiššōḵ* requires a direct object in the accusative case, this is not so with *yiššaḵ*. In *nāšal* the intransitive meaning is probably the primary if not the only correct meaning; [2] for as used of clothes there is no more need for it than for *lābaš*/*lāḇēš* 'wore' to be regarded as transitive,[3] while the use of the Qal of clearing away nations [4] is probably an error of punctuation for the Piʿēl. Obviously, *nāšaq* must be regarded as intransitive, as the object is almost always introduced by a preposition in preference to the accusative case, although it can also be treated as a transitive verb; and this is supported by the fact that the Acc. *našāqu* is usually employed in the II i theme (Piʿēl), although here too the I i theme (Qal) is not unknown in a transitive sense. In *yipṭar* the *a* is due to the fact that in the only passage in which the imperfect tense occurs the meaning is intransitive; [5] but, as the Acc. *paṭāru* 'to set free' and the Hebr. *pāṭar* 'set free' are elsewhere transitive, the apparently intransitive use must have sprung from the ellipse of some easily supplied object which it governed as a transitive verb,[6] so that the vocalization with *a* instead of *ō* is probably a Massoretic error.[7]

Finally, the following verbs take both *ō* and *a* or *e* in the imperfect tense:

ḥālaš 'prostrated'; 'was prostrated'	*ḥānan* 'was favourably inclined'; 'treated favourably'	*pāšaṭ* 'stripped off'
ḥāmam 'was hot'	*yāṣaq* 'poured out'; 'flowed'	*śārar* 'was a prince'
	nāḏaḏ 'fled, wandered, fluttered'	

The proper form of the imperfect tense of *nādad* is that with *a* which, however, occurs only once,[8] while the alternative form with *ō* or *ô* is due to the analogy of *nûḏ* 'to wander, to flutter'; for hollow verbs with medial *w* quite often have *ô* instead of *û* in that tense, as already said.[9] Again, neither form of the imperfect of *śārar* is correctly vocalized; for the vocalization of *wayyāśar* [10] is that of an intransitive hollow verb [11] and that

[1] Cp. Acc. *iššuk* 'bit' beside *iššik* 'set up' for a similar differentiation of two roots identical in form; in the first the influence of *k*, in the second that of *š* is followed.

[2] The post-Bibl. Hebr. *hiššîl* 'cast off' implies an intransitive Qal.

[3] Cp. Arab. *nasala* 'fell out' (with feathers as subject), and 'moulted' (with feathers as indirect object).

[4] Deut. 7. 1, 22; cp. 2 Ki. *16*. 6.

[5] 1 Sam. *19*. 10. The Bab. *paṭāru* is used similarly in the letters from Tall-al-'Amârna.

[6] *E.g.* 'he loosed (*sc.* his beast)' or 'he loosed (*sc.* the cords of his tent)' or the like = 'he departed.'

[7] Cp. Bab. *ipṭur* and so on (s. Knudtzon, *A.-T.* 1491), which militates against supposing that the *a* has arisen out of an original *i* due to the following sonant *r*.

[8] In Gen. *31*. 40.

[9] S. pp. 64–65.

[10] Judg. *9*. 22.

[11] Cp. *wayyāsar* 'and he turned aside.'

verbs with *ē* (*e*) in the imperfect tense, which are usually referred to the Hip̱ʿîl but which he prefers to regard as forms of the Qal with *i* or *ē* (*e*), as they are found otherwise only in that theme. These verbs, classed according to this vowel, are the following:

(i) with *i*:

ṭāman 'hid'[1] (Arab. *yaṭmiru*) *pāraḥ* 'flourished'[2]
yāšar 'was straight'[3] (Arab. *yayširu*) *rāṣas* 'crushed'[4]
ʿāram 'was shrewd'[5] (Arab. *yaʿru/i/amu*)

(ii) with *ē* (*e*):

'āmaṣ 'was strong'[6] *hālal* 'shone'[7] (Arab. *yahillu*)
'āṣal 'set apart'[8] *sāḵaḵ* 'screened'[9]
gālal 'rolled away'[10] *ṣālal* 'tingled'[11] (Arab. *yaṣillu*)
gānan 'shielded'[12] (Arab. *yajinnu*)

At first sight it is tempting to reject all these forms as Massoretic freaks, but their very number gives pause to hasty alterations of the vocalization; further, as Barth[13] has observed, they are confirmed by the two facts that the place-name *Yaʿzēr*[14] is transliterated *Ιαζηρ*[15] by the LXX, and that in more than half of them the corresponding Arabic verb has *i* in the same tense.[16] It is at once clear that the meaning can have nothing to do with the vocalization of these verbs, since exactly half are transitive and half are intransitive; it must therefore depend on the nature or form of the root itself. Barth[17] indeed suggests as the rule governing all these forms of the imperfect tense that a primitive *i* > *ē* is preserved when the prefix is sharpened (as in *yittēn*) or lengthened (as in *yēlēḏ*) and when the prefix has *a* (as in *ya'ṭem*, *yaʿrim*, *yāg̱ēn*), which is also the case with verbs beginning with *'* (as in *yō'ḇēḏ*). These rules, however, are too complex and, moreover, merely describe without explaining the phenomenon under discussion, and they are quite invalid in the case of those Accadian verbs which exhibit the same phenomenon. The same reason must accordingly be sought to explain the peculiar vowel in both languages and this can hardly be any other than the liquid and/or sibilant letter which occurs

[1] 2 Ki. *7*. 8 (*yaṭmīnû*).
[2] Jb. *14*. 9 (*yaprīᵃḥ*); Prov. *14*. 11 (*yaprîᵃḥ*); Ps. *92*. 14 (*yaprîḥû*).
[3] Prov. *4*. 25 (*yayšīrû*). [4] Jud. *9*. 53 (*wattāriṣ*).
[5] 1 Sam. *23*. 22; Prov. *15*. 5, *19*. 25 (*yaʿrīm*).
[6] Ps. *27*. 14, *31*. 25 (*ya'amēṣ*).
[7] Jb. *31*. 26 (*yāhēl*); Jb. *41*. 10 (*tāhel*); Is. *13*. 10 (*yāhēllû*).
[8] Numb. *11*. 25 (*wayyâṣel*).
[9] Ps. *91*. 4 (*yāseḵ*); Ex. *40*. 21 (*wayyāseḵ*); Ps. *5*. 12 (*tāsēḵ*).
[10] Gen. *29*. 10 (*wayyāgel*). [11] 1 Sam. *3*. 11 (*tᵉṣilleynāh*).
[12] Is. *31*. 5, Zech. *9*. 15, *12*. 8 (*yāg̱ēn*).
[13] In *Nb.S.S.* I. 103–104.
[14] Incorrectly *Yaʿzêr* (1 Chron. *6*. 66, *26*. 31); cp. Acc. *Yaẖziru*.
[15] Also Ιαζειρ in Lucian (Josh. *13*. 25).
[16] Cp. Arab. *yaʿḏiru* 'he excuses,' the imperfect form of the cognate verb from which the Hebr. *Yaʿzēr* is derived.
[17] In *Z.D.M.G.* XLIII. 189–190.

in the second and/or third place in the root of 12 out of 13 of these verbs; amongst these is included *sāḵaḵ*, as its *s* comes into immediate contact with and is therefore responsible for the *ē* in the imperfect *yāsēḵ*.[1] Barth adds also *'āṭam* [2] to the list, but this may be not Qal but Hipʿîl (although the explanation of the jussive form is a different matter),[3] as the Massoretes have taken it; for the cognate verbs (Syr. *'eṭam* 'was deaf,' [4] Arab. *'aṭima* 'was contracted'),[5] suggest that the Hebr. *'āṭam* may have meant in the Qal 'was heavy' or 'was slow,' [6] rather than 'stopped,' when the Hipʿîl will have had a causative sense.[7]

Clearly, then, in Accadian the phonetic principle is still strong, while in Hebrew it exercises, except in the case of guttural verbs, but little influence, having given place in most cases to the semantic principle. This point will be made clear by a glance at certain verbs which seem at first sight clearly to violate it, as set out in the following lists:

(i) with imperfect *yiqṭōl*:

	dāraš 'sought'	
'āzar 'guided'	*hāras* 'tore down'	*'āšar* 'tithed'
'āsar 'bound'	*ḥāraš* 'ploughed'	*pāraṣ* 'broke through'
bāzar 'scattered'	*nāṣar* 'guarded'	*pāraś* 'spread out'
bāṣar 'cut off'	*'āzar* 'helped'	*qāṣar* 'reaped'
gāzal 'stole'	*'ānaš* 'fined'	*qāšar* 'bound'
gāzar 'divided'	*'āṣar* 'restrained'	*šāsas* 'despoiled'

(ii) with imperfect *yiqṭal*:

dāḇēq 'clung'	*'āgaḇ* 'lusted'	*rāqaḇ* 'rotted'
ḥāḵam 'was wise'	*rāṭaḇ* 'was moist'	*šāḵaḇ* 'lay down'
	rāḵaḇ 'rode' [8]	

It is at once evident that, if the phonetic principle were followed, the verbs in the first list would have $i > a$ and those in the second list $u > \bar{o}$ in the imperfect tense; the reason why this is not so can only be that the semantic principle has here prevailed.

Finally, care must be taken to remark that the various languages may not all follow the same line of development but may each go their own way: for example, the Acc. *emē/ādu* 'to stand, to put' makes *ēmid* by vowel-harmony, while the

[1] S. pp. 64–65, 67–68. [2] Ps. *58*. 5 (cp. Arab. *ya'ṭimu*).
[3] It is an (apocopated) aorist tense used with gnomic force (s. pp. 139–141).
[4] Brockelmann, *Lex. Syr.* 14. [5] Freytag, *Lex. Arab.-Lat.* I. 41–42.
[6] Thus *'ōṭēm 'oznô* (Is. *33*. 15, Prov. *21*. 13) and *'ōṭēm śᵉpāṯāyw* (Prov. *17*. 28) will mean respectively 'slow of hearing' and 'slow of speech.'
[7] At the same time there seems to have been a transitive Hebr. *'āṭam* 'contracted' corresponding with the Arab. *'aṭama* (cp. post-Bibl. Hebr. *'āṭam*) 'covered over' (*l.c.*), as the passive participle of the Qal occurs three times according to the Massoretic vocalization (1 Ki. *6*. 4; Ezek. *40*. 16, *41*. 16, 26); this may have been a secondary formation from the primitive intransitive root.
[8] Cp. Acc. *irkab* (s. p. 61).

VII

Special Terminations with Verbs

It remains to discuss the origin and purpose of the vocalic and consonantal terminations attached to many verbal forms; for they are as diverse in origin as they are varied in use.

In Accadian the permansive *qaṭil* normally has no vowel-ending but an *-a* and sometimes an *-i* or a *-u* appear, especially in early forms of proper names;[1] an *-a* is normally added to the perfect forms in classical Arabic and Ethiopic and is found in Hebrew and Aramaic only before pronominal suffixes (*e.g.* Hebr. *qᵉṭālanî* and Aram. *qaṭlanî*; cp. Arab. *qátalanî* and Eth. *qatálanī*). The origin of this vowel has been much discussed and various reasons to account for it have been put forward. The simplest explanation is that it is due to the difficulty of ending on a final consonant without giving utterance to a furtive vowel; for it is a well-known tendency of primitive peoples to slip in a vowel between two consonants whether between syllables or words, and the Semites (especially the Arabs) show elsewhere evident traces of this tendency. Whether this short vowel was original or, as Nix[2] thinks, an euphonic addition made only in those languages which disliked a consonantal ending, is hard to determine; but as traces of it are found in all the Semitic languages, it is preferable to regard it as a primitive element. It is another question why it has survived in full use in Arabic and Ethiopic but has almost vanished from Accadian, Hebrew and Aramaic. It seems that it was dropped in Accadian because *qaṭil*, being in origin a noun, was used for the most part predicatively; thus when it preceded the subject, usually a pronoun, it coalesced with it and so lost its final vowel or, when it followed it, it closed the sentence and therefore was put in the abruptest, *i.e.* the absolute, state which was characterized by the absence of any ending. In Hebrew and Aramaic it fell away because of the well-attested tendency of those languages to get rid of all final short vowels, surviving only in certain forms for the sake of euphony. It is, however, remarkable that a final *-a* is attached to the permansive

[1] In ordinary verbs, as in *marṣa* 'he is ill' (Harper, *A.B.L.* IV. *347*, Obv. 6, 8), it is probably an orthographic freak, due to the fact that every consonant must carry a vowel with it in the Accadian syllabary; incidentally such forms conform the accentuation of the Acc. *qáṭil*.

[2] In *Z.A.* X. 178–179.

state in a number of early Accadian proper names, such as *Bēlum-nāda*. Albright [1] suggests that it is preserved in such cases with a view to making the hollow root conform to the common Semitic triconsonantal noun; but this explanation will not account for the same final vowel in such names as *Ammi-ṣaduga* and *Abad-Ištara*. Schultze, as Brockelmann [2] remarks, thinks it identical with the interjectional and demonstrative *hā-*, with which the Aramaic *-â* attached to emphatic nouns is akin, and Speiser [3] connects it with the accusative ending on the ground that *qariba* 'he is near' is in fact a predicate and that the predicate stands in the accusative case; but this militates against the fact that the predicate properly stands in the (nominative) absolute state in Accadian and in the accusative case only in Arabic, which is a relatively late language, nor does it explain why other names of similar formation terminate in *-i* or *-u*: for example, *Šamaš-ḫazir* and *Šamaš-ḫaziru* beside *Ili-ḫaziri* in Old-Babylonian and *Ašir-dān* beside *Ašir-dāni* in Old-Assyrian texts. The simplest reason seems again to be the dislike of ending on a consonant, so that, even where the absolute state might be expected, any short vowel was added for the sake of euphony, either *-a* on the analogy of the primitive verbal ending or through vowel-harmony or *-u* as the nominative termination (though improperly used with predicative forms) or *-i* under the influence of assimilation. This loose use of vowel-endings indeed becomes increasingly common in Accadian texts as time goes on, whether it is due to euphonic reasons or orthographic difficulties. In Arabic, which notoriously preserves many primitive elements and which in any case has no objection to final short vowels, it will be a relic of the primitive Semitic speech, and in this respect as in many others Ethiopic for obvious reasons follows suit.

In Accadian the ending *-u* is properly attached to verbs in relative and other dependent clauses, namely only when they stand in the subjunctive mood. Knudtzon [4] indeed has already rightly suggested that this was nothing else than the termination *-u(m)* of the nominative case, since the permansive *qaṭil* was nominal or adjectival in origin and could indeed be inflected adjectivally throughout the history of the language; it is natural, therefore, to suppose that when it performed the function of a verb, just as when it served as a predicate, it was left uninflected like a noun or adjective in a similar position, but that when it stood in a relative clause—namely, when its function was the same as that of a qualifying adjective—it was treated

[1] In *J.B.L.* LIV. 197[77]. [2] In *G.V.G.S.S.* I. § 262a.
[3] In *J.A.O.S.* LVI. 35. [4] In *Z.A.* VI. 419[1].

Finally Landsberger [1] has shown that this *-a* has often, even in early Babylonian texts, what he calls a 'ventive' force, as seen in the distinction between *illik* 'he went' and *illika* 'he came,' and this suggests that it too is deictic in origin, though often used as an emphatic and even merely as a pausal ending. In Hebrew, however, it has no 'ventive' force and was commonly preserved only as a cohortative ending, though still continuing to be used in poetry simply as an emphatic termination. Accordingly, as an Assyrian king could say equally well *šallasunu utīr* or *uteirra* 'I brought back their spoil' [2] so a Hebrew poet could say either *'erdᵉp̄āh* or *'erdôp̄ 'ōyᵉḇay* 'I pursued mine enemies,' [3] since the verb is not in the imperfect but in the preterite tense [4]; but it is significant that this and all the other instances of the Hebrew *-āh* referring to past time are in poetical passages,[5] where archaisms are *a priori* likely.

In Arabic the imperfect tense takes *-u* in the indicative and *-a* in the subjunctive mood, and it is difficult to remove these two endings out of the main course of development of the Semitic verb; they must therefore be explained in the light of the same endings in Accadian. There, as already shown, the ending *-u* on the one hand was transferred from the permansive state by false analogy to the present and preterite tenses, to which it was added in dependent clauses regarded as adjectives standing predicatively in the nominative case, even when attached to a purely verbal form; with the inflectional decay of the language, however, this *-u* came to be freely attached to any verbal form, whether in the indicative or in the subjunctive mood. Thus what in Accadian had originally been restricted to relative, *i.e.* adjectival, clauses passed over into Arabic as a sign of a purely verbal predicate but was erroneously retained only with the indicative mood. The ending *-a* on the other hand was originally deictic or demonstrative [6] and as such could be used either in main or less often in dependent clauses in place of the proper subjunctive *-u*; [7] and this usage too increased with the lapse of syntactical exactitude as time went on. In the same way, then, this ending

[1] In *Z.A.* XXXV. 114–116. Hebrew seems to have preserved a tendency to a similar distinction between *lēḵ* 'go' and *lᵉḵāh* 'come' (s. Brown & Driver & Briggs, *Hebr. Lex.* under *hālaḵ* I. 1 *c* and 5 *f*).

[2] Budge & King, *Ā.K.A.* I. 73, v. 51–53 (and so often in Assyrian inscriptions with this and similar verbs). It makes no difference to the argument that in this particular phrase the termination has perhaps a ventive force.

[3] 2 Sam. *22*. 38=Ps. *18*. 38, where the following verb shows that the reference is to past time.

[4] S. pp. 120–121, 141–142.

[5] S. R. Driver, *Tenses*, 58–59.

[6] Cp. Bauer & Leander, *Hist. Gr. d. hebr. Spr.* I. 273, where the ending *-a* as attached to *yaqtul* is explained as an interjection marking purpose or intention.

[7] Delitzsch, *Ass. Gramm.* 363–364; cp. Zimmern, *V.G.S.S.* 117–118.

passed over into Arabic, where it was restricted to a use which had not belonged to it at any rate according to its origin but which had been acquired by it in the course of ages. Both terminations served also to distinguish these forms of the verb from the jussive *yaqtul*, and this fact may have helped to ensure their preservation. The use of these endings, then, in Arabic can be explained as an extension of the uses to which they had come to be put in Accadian, and the explanation of the native Arab grammarians of the *-u* in the indicative *yaqtulu* as a nominative and of the *-a* in the subjunctive *yaqtula* as an accusative ending may be regarded as an artificial attempt to account for something of which the origin was lost in the mists of antiquity ; yet they hit the truth to this extent that the *-u* had indeed originally been the mark of the nominative case, even when transferred to a verbal form, and that the *-a* was indeed directional, like the accusative ending, being the mark of a dependent clause which limited the operation of the main clause to a person or thing possessing the qualities described or to the manner set forth in it.

The energic *-n* [1] is easily explained, being of the same nature as the plural *-n* in origin. For, as the idea of intensity or multiplicity is imparted to the noun by prolonging its final vowel by nasalization, so weight is imparted to the verb by the nasalization of the final sound, and this process tends naturally to a full consonant, namely *-n*, though not in the strict sense a consonantal sound. Thus too it may be added to give stress to various pronouns and may be used elsewhere, whereby its properly emphatic force acquires a virtually deictic significance.

[1] It occurs also very commonly in Ugaritian, where however its force requires elucidation (s. Montgomery & Harris, *Ras Shamra*, 23–24).

and the plural endings of the nominative and accusative cases were or became identical, leaving the construction ambiguous [1] The imperfections, then, of the case-endings as indicative of the construction and indeed their rapid decay nullified this safeguard and so are one of the causes of the scarcity of the active use of *qaṭil*. In the West, on the other hand, the case-endings had disappeared even before the evolution of the classical language, and it was therefore imperative that, if the noun could give no indication of the construction, the verb should do so; for thus the sense depended on it in the vast majority of cases. Consequently an active *qatal* was developed out of *qatil* by a change of vowel based on the accordance of the nature of the vowel with the meaning required to be expressed; at the same time too as *qāṭēl* lost its active significance by the development of the active *qāṭal*, it lost also its passive significance by the development of the internal passive *quṭ(ṭ)al* of which traces remain not only in the tablets from Tall-al-ʿAmârna but also in the Old Testament. Thus the Hebrew *qāṭēl* was able to remain a purely and almost exclusively stative or intransitive force.[2] In meaning, inasmuch as *qāṭēl* referred to a state which had already arisen before the moment of speaking, it was natural that the newly created *qāṭal* should describe at any rate primarily an act which had already occurred. Yet it retained enough of the old universal sense of the original *qatil* from which it had diverged to be also employed not only for the description of facts which have formerly taken place but are still of constant recurrence and hence are matters of common experience (namely, to perform the function of a gnomic aorist) but also with reference to future events, although this use was in practice confined to poetic and the kindred prophetic language and certain legal phrases.[3] This usage

[1] The confusion was increased by the additional of modal terminations to the 3rd. person of the permansive state (s. Meissner, *K.A.G.* § 52. c).

[2] Torczyner (in *Z.D.M.G.* LXIV. 300) has remarked that originally all Accadian verbs must have been indifferently transitive and intransitive; for many (such as *abātu* 'to be ruined' and 'to destroy' and *emēdu* 'to stand' and 'to set up') show clear traces of this state in other parts than the equivocal *qaṭil*; and it may then be added that this must also have once been so also in Hebrew, as such verbs as *sāmak* 'leaned' and 'upheld' prove (s. p. 52). Sometimes, too, verbs have gone the one way in the one language and the other way in the other language, as a comparison of the Acc. *ippul* 'felled' with the Hebr. *yippōl* 'fell' shows. Further, when the distinction is made in the Semitic languages, it is not between transitive and intransitive but rather between active and stative verbs, as Lambert (in *J.As.* VIII. xv. 166) has shown; the former describe an activity and may or may not require a limiting or defining accusative case (*i.e.* they may be either transitive or neutral), the latter describe a state and do not require definition (although the part affected is sometimes added in the accusative case). Thus Brockelmann (*G.V.G.S.S.* II. 133–141) is probably right in abandoning the view that the Semitic language in primitive times can have distinguished active and passive forms of the verb.

[3] Kautzsch & Cowley, *Hebr. Gramm.* § 106 m–n (s. pp. 116–117).

however was rare and almost, if not quite, died out at a relatively early date; for while the conception of a form of the verb having a universal range is possible in regard to the description of a state, it is not so easily compatible with the description of an act. Thus *qāṭal* became a pure tense restricted almost entirely to past time, while *qāṭēl* lingered on with a permansive force appropriate to the description of states and endowed with much of the universal range of the primitive archetype from which it was descended.

Hebrew, then, having a perfect, had no great need of a separate preterite tense but only of one describing the reverse of completed, *i.e.* incomplete, action. One problem, then, is to discover why Hebrew did not adopt a form derived from *yaqatal* for the tense of incomplete action (as Accadian formed *iqaṭa/il* for a present-future tense) instead of one derived from *yaqtul* (from which Accadian derived *iqṭul* as a preterite tense). This is all the more striking, because *iqaṭa/il* is of regular occurrence in the letters from Tall-al-ʿAmârna. Torczyner,[1] therefore, is perhaps right in suggesting that Hebrew may once have possessed such a tense but must have lost it in the pre-literary period, as no trace of it survives in the written language. If this form, which is as often as not there written *(y)iqaṭ(ṭ)a/il* (with a double consonant to indicate the accent), had passed into or survived in Hebrew, the form of the Qal imperfect *yᵉqaṭṭēl* would have been indistinguishable from that of the Piʿēl; for *yidabbir* would have become *yᵉḏabbēr*, *yagarrib* (for *yaqarrib*) would have become *yᵉqārēḇ*, *(y)išaʼil* would have become *yᵉšāʼēl* and so on.[2] This suggestion is supported by the fact that the old passive forms of the Qal which were indicated solely by internal modification of the vowel fell into desuetude at an early period because they were indistinguishable from the passive forms of Piʿēl (Puʿal) and of Hipʿîl (Hopʿal).[3] In both cases the same cause was operative, namely the desire to avoid a confusion between the Qal and the derived themes where there was no sharp distinction of meaning; for, as the active Qal and the Piʿēl, so the passive Qal and the Puʿal or Hopʿal must in many cases have been almost if not quite identical in

[1] In *Z.D.M.G.* LXVI. 88.

[2] Thus the primitive passives *ʼukal* 'it was eaten' and *yutan* 'it is given' become *ʼukkāl* (for *ʼukkal* through a misunderstanding of the form) and *yuttan* respectively with a doubling of the medial consonant to preserve the preceding short vowel (s. p. 93).

[3] In the letters from Tall-al-ʿAmârna there is a passive imperfect *yuq(a)ṭal* (of which there seem to be traces also in early Aramaic and which is fully preserved in classical Arabic): for example, *yudan* (Hebr. *yuttan*) 'it is given.' Of the perfect passive *quṭal*, of which too traces have survived in classical Hebrew (cp. *ʼukkāl* 'it has been eaten'), there is no trace in these letters, obviously because the intransitive (permansive) *qaṭil* could be used with a passive force (Böhl, *Spr. d. Amarnabr.* 60–63).

qualified sense, to direct him rather to some particular locality, some previously marked spot, where and where alone the assertion may be found verified.' [1] Of these two theories to account for the change of accent the first implies too artificial an idea to be in the least degree convincing, at any rate as applied to a very early if not primitive construction; the second, which is plausible in the case of the imperfect but seems forced in that of the perfect, is open to the serious objection that it necessitates two different causes to explain what are at bottom only two parts or aspects of one and the same phenomenon. Nor does either theory account for the difference in the form of the conjunction with the perfect from that which it assumes with the imperfect tense.

Equally unsatisfactory is the current explanation of this construction itself. It is that in the first case 'the imperfect represents action as nascent: accordingly, when combined with a conjunction connecting the event introduced by it with a point already reached by the narrative, it represents it as the continuation or development of the part which came before it.' [2] In the second case it is supposed to have been evoked by the opposite idiom with the imperfect, since there are many well-known aspects under which these tenses are contrasted, and it is then suggested that 'the *wāw* possesses really in this connection a demonstrative significance, being equivalent to "then" or "so"; in this capacity, by a pointed reference to some preceding verb, it limits the possible realization of the action introduced by it to those instances in which it can be treated as a direct consequence of the event thus referred to.' [3] These attempts to solve the problem are confronted by various difficulties. In general, like one at any rate of the theories put forward to explain the change of accent, they seem to explain the two parts of the problem in different ways. Moreover, they seem also to imply a cross-division in the conception assumed to underlie the functions of the two tenses, namely they not only postulate as one distinction between them that the perfect describes a completed act while the imperfect describes incomplete action, but they also introduce the new idea that the imperfect describes nascent or emergent action; yet every action, whether incomplete or complete, is in some sense nascent or emergent, *i.e.* it has arisen out of certain precedent conditions which will have been described by a preceding verb in the narration of the story. At the same time the nascent act described as such by the imperfect may in itself be complete and ought therefore from that point of view to be described by a perfect tense. Thus the theory does not

[1] S. R. Driver, *Tenses*, 117–118. [2] *Ibid.* 70–73. [3] *Ibid.* 117–118.

explain why Hebrew should apparently arbitrarily abandon its usual classification of acts as complete or incomplete in favour of a different and at times inconsistent classification of them as nascent or emergent. In particular, a number of idiomatic uses of both tenses are only with great difficulty explained, if indeed they can be explained, on the usual theories concerning the Semitic tenses. Thus in Hebrew the (apparently imperfect) *yiqṭōl* is at times employed in a purely preterite sense. This occurs principally after the particle *'āz* 'then' as well as generally after *ṭerem* 'before' and occasionally after *'aḏ* 'until'; and this construction has been explained on the theory of emergent or nascent action in such a way that, for example, *'āz yᵉḏabbēr* is interpreted as meaning not so much 'then he spoke' as 'then he went on to speak,' when indeed such an explanation is more or less plausible. But the theory becomes a *reductio ad absurdum* as applied to the preterite use of *yiqṭōl* in poetry: for example, it is hopelessly forced to explain *Śārāh tᵉḥôlelᵉḵem* 'S. (who) travailed with you'[1] as meaning properly 'S. (who) went on to travail with you.' Indeed, there are many passages where any such idea is totally inapplicable.[2] Similarly, there are constructions in the cognate languages which cannot be satisfactorily explained on any such theories: *e.g.* why in Arabic *lam* 'not' and *lammâ* 'not yet' when negating events in past time as well as *'iḏ* 'then' in reference to past time require (the apparently jussive) *yaqtul*, as in *lam*(*mâ*) *ta'lam* 'thou didst not (yet) know.'[3] Nor do such explanations account for many of the constructions found with the perfect tense. Thus in Hebrew the perfect tense appears often to be applied to future events; this, since the most frequent occurrence of it is in the writings of the prophets, has been styled the 'prophetic perfect' and is explained on the theory that 'it imparts to descriptions of the future a forcible and expressive touch of reality, and reproduces vividly the certainty with which the occurrence of a yet future event is contemplated by the speaker.'[4] As used by the prophets, the phenomenon is thus probably rightly explained, but that this is not its origin is suggested by the fact that it occurs in numerous passages where there is no trace of prophetic vividness or where it is entirely out of place: for example, in such questions in Hebrew as *'aḏ māṯay mē'antā* 'how long wilt thou have refused?' where the imperfect tense

[1] Is. *51.* 2, where Graetz alters *tᵉḥôlelᵉḵem* into *ḥôlᵉlaṯᵉḵem*; this facile emendation fails to account for the corruption of an easy into a difficult reading and is disproved by many parallel usages (cp. Jb. *3.* 3), especially in the works of the prophets (s. pp. 120–121, 139–142).

[2] S. R. Driver, *Tenses*, 30–33.

[3] Wright, *Arab. Gramm.* II. 12, 22–23.

[4] S. R. Driver, *Tenses*, 18–21.

the Hebrew verb, then, in the construction with consecutive *wāw* is that of the primitive Semitic speech as exhibited in the Accadian language and must therefore be regarded not as a peculiarity invented by the Hebrews but as an archaism surviving from the common proto-Semitic speech.[1] Both forms, however, as examples cited below clearly show,[2] could be used in their original senses without the warning particle. When the old permansive form of the verb was thus used alone with a future sense in poetry and the language of prophecy, it came to be incorrectly accented like the true perfect *šāḵántā* 'thou hast dwelt.' In some persons (singular and plural third person, plural first and second persons) there was already no distinction in the accentuation, and it was natural that the other persons (singular first and second persons) should follow suit and adopt the normal accentuation of the western Semitic verb.[3] This process was further helped by the fact that the accentuation in certain classes of weak verbs (*i.e.* those with a final ʼ and a final *h*) in the East as well as in the West had always taken the accent on the second or final syllable of the root: for example, the Hebr. *nāśā́ṯā* 'thou hast lifted up' and *wᵉnāśā́ṯā* 'and thou wilt lift up' as well as *rāḇîṯā* 'thou art great' and *wᵉrāḇîṯā* 'and thou wilt be great' are both accented after the model of the Acc. *naṣā́ta*[4] 'thou dost lift up' and *rabā́ta*[5] 'thou art great' respectively. Thus two anomalies in Hebrew accentuation, that of two classes of weak verbs with consecutive *wāw* in the perfect and that of the 'prophetic perfect' after the model of a true perfect tense instead of a permansive form of universal application, are simultaneously explained. So too the original accentuation of the preterite tense as shown by the Acc. *íbni* 'he built' is preserved with the verbal consecutive *wāw* in the Hebr. *wayyíḇn* 'and he built';

[1] Brockelmann (*G.V.G.S.S.* II. 150¹) objects to the view, at which Bauer has already hinted (in *B.A.S.S.* VIII. i. 37), that the accentuation of the verb with consecutive *wāw* is an archaism, on the ground that, if it were so, the *a* would become *šᵉwâ* under the first syllable in the perfect (as in *qᵉṭaltem*); and he might have added that the *ō* or other final vowel in the imperfect would *ex hypothesi* have been shortened (as sometimes after *'al* and perhaps also other particles when closely linked to the following word). The answer to this objection is that it is just because the accentuation was archaic that the shortening of these vowels did not take place; these forms of the verb were not indigenous but were taken over, as it were, bodily into Hebrew. Consequently, since there was a full vowel in the first syllable of the proto-Semitic verb, as the Acc. *qáṭlāta* shows, the Hebrew *wᵉqāṭaltā́* retained the full vowel as *a* in the same place; and in the same way the primitive accent as seen in the Acc. *iqṭul* reappeared in the consecutive forms of weak verbs, while *wayyiqṭōl* was exempted from the rules of accentuation and was assimilated to the imperfect *yiqṭōl*.

[2] S. pp. 120–121, 132–144.

[3] So the Hebr. *qāṭál* is an imperfect synthesis of Eastern and Western forms; for the long *a* reflects the accented *a* of the Acc. *qáṭil* and the accent on the short *a* corresponds with that on the Aram. *qᵉṭál*. Other forms of the perfect tense may be similarly explained.

[4] Contracted from *našiāta*.

[5] Contracted from *rabiāta*.

but beside this, the proper preterite form, there is also occasionally found *wayyiḇnéh* 'and he built,'[1] formed incorrectly with the imperfect *yiḇnéh* 'he was building.' This confusion shows that at an early stage the true distinction between the Eastern preterite *yáqtul* and the Western imperfect *yaqtúl* had been forgotten owing to the similarity of the two forms; for the distinction between them, which from the beginning had depended in the strong verb solely on the accent, had easily become obscured, and the consequent error had been extended even to the extent of obliterating the distinction in form between the two tenses in the weak verb. In other words, the accentuation of the preterite *wayyiqṭṓl* 'and he killed' was due to the model of the imperfect *yiqṭṓl* 'he was killing,' with which it was incorrectly identified; and the analogy of this mistake led to the use of the imperfect *yiḇnéh* in *wayyiḇnéh* 'and he built' with the sense of the preterite *yíḇn* as correctly employed in *wayyíḇn* 'and he built.' Nor is such an error in the least degree improbable; for exactly the same thing has occurred in the use of the imperfect *ta'ăśeh* in *'al ta'ăśeh* for the jussive *ta'aś* in *'al ta'aś* 'do not do.'[2] Again, in Arabic the preterite *yaqtul* as properly employed in *lam ya'ti* 'he did not come'[3] has been confused with or given way to the imperfect *yaqtulu* in such phrases as *fa'aḫruju* 'so I went out.'[4] The assumption of some such confusion between two closely similar forms in the course of many centuries seems at any rate as simple a solution of the complex problem presented by the divers and often contradictory usages of *yaqtul(u)* as the endeavour to explain them all on the assumption, often far-fetched, of a common underlying sense such as that of nascence or emergence.

This theory has the additional advantage that it explains why different conjunctions are used with the perfect and imperfect tenses in this construction. In Accadian, on the one hand, the conjunction *u* was employed to connect nouns and adjectives and nominal expressions generally, amongst which were naturally and properly included permansive forms of the verb, inasmuch as they were of course of nominal origin; on the other hand, the enclitic *-ma* was properly employed in verbal clauses, where it served to connect a series of verbs whether they described simultaneous or successive events. For this *-ma* was in origin no conjunction but an emphasizing particle attached to the word on which it was desired to lay stress,[5] especially to

[1] Bauer & Leander, *Hist. Gramm. d. hebr. Spr.* I. § 57 u′.

[2] Cp. Jer. *40.* 16, where the K. is *ta'aś* and the Q. is *ta'ăśeh* (cp. 1 Sam. *13.* 12). The imperative *hērā'ēh* 'show thyself' (1 Ki. *18.* 1) is an extreme example of this tendency.

[3] Qur'ân *Sûr. 23.* 70 (s. pp. 120–121, 138–139).

[4] S. pp. 121–123.

[5] Cp. Ungnad in *B.A.S.S.* V. 713–716.

Accadian present *iqáṭal*, and that *qāṭál* alone in the time-sphere of a perfect participle is a new formation of the West-Semitic style. That this construction too is an archaism may be at once conceded, inasmuch as it is inexplicable so long as a belief in the absolute perfect significance of *qāṭal* is retained, but the explanation of the future use of *qāṭal* by postulating its ultimate identity with *iqáṭal* cannot be accepted for reasons not only of development but also of use. Moreover, two Accadian examples will at once show how this construction originated. In *ammīni lā tākul lā talti-ma* [1] *lā balṭāta* 'why didst thou not eat (and) not drink indeed? Thou shalt not live' [2] the question and the command are set independently beside one another and the construction is co-ordinate; the preterite tense refers to past time and the permansive state has a future reference. In 'I shall leave (*ītizib*) the city and depart (*u paṭrāti*)' [3] and 'the gift of her husband together with his present she shall take and (*talakkie-ma*) [4] she shall carry away (*ablat*),' [5] however, both verbal forms have a future force, and the Accadian permansive state is used precisely like the Hebrew perfect tense with consecutive *wāw*; but, while the Accadian permansive state has come to be regarded as a verb in such a construction and therefore is introduced by the verbal *-ma* (in so far as that may be regarded as a connecting particle), the Hebrew perfect tense is still treated as a noun and is introduced by the originally nominal *u*; [6] this fact, together with a consideration of passages such as those just quoted, show clearly that the use of *qâṭal* with consecutive *wāw* with reference to future time is a genuine development of that of *qátil* in a universal sense.

Finally, the theory here put forward offers a simple explanation of the other facts for which the old attempts to solve the problem have accounted but unsatisfactorily. Thus the use of *qāṭal* in reference to future time and with an optative force is seen to be a relic of the universal sense, of which the Accadian *qaṭil* has preserved clear traces, of the primitive *qatil*; this is made clear by a few examples from Accadian, such as *qaqqadša pattu* 'her head shall be uncovered' [7] and *eli rubī u šarri dameiq* 'unto prince and king may it be pleasing!' [8] So, too, the use

[1] For *tašti*.

[2] Jensen in Schrader's *K.B.* VI. i. 98–99 $_{31-32}$.

[3] Knudtzon, *A.-T. 82.* 43–44.

[4] For *talaqi/e*.

[5] Peiser in Schrader's *K.B.* IV. 322–323, iv. 16–19.

[6] The Accadian usage however is fluctuating, as shown by such a sentence as *bītāti . . . altegi-mi u aplāku-mi* 'saying: the houses . . . I took and I have been paid' (Pfeiffer, *E.N.* II. *21.* 26–29).

[7] Driver & Miles, *Ass. L. 40.* 67.

[8] The particle *lū* is usually prefixed to *qaṭil* when it has an optative force (s. pp. 33–34).

of *yiqṭōl* in reference to purely past time in poetry and after certain particles is seen to be not an abuse of the imperfect of incomplete action but a survival of the preterite *yaqtul*, which remained in full force in the Accadian *iqṭul*, from the primitive Semitic speech. That *yiqṭōl* in such a connection is not in any sense imperfect but preterite is shown by the fact that *'āz dibber* is no less correct than *'āz yᵉḏabbēr* as meaning 'then he spoke'; as there is no idea of nascence or emergence in *dibber*, so there is no reason to expect it in *yᵉḏabbēr*. Again, there is little if any distinction of time between the two tenses in 'pangs did seize (*'āḥaz*) the inhabitants of Philistia'[1] and 'the bucks of Moab, trembling did seize them (*yō'ḥăzēmû*),[2] or between those in *yôm 'iwwāleḏ bô* 'the day whereon I was born'[3] and *hayyôm 'ăšer yullaḏtî bô yôm 'ăšer yᵉlāḏaṯnî 'immî* 'the day whereon I was born, (the) day when my mother bare me';[4] in the apparent imperfect as in the perfect tenses there is no idea of incipience but only a purely past sense, and these may therefore be explained as archaic preterite tenses hardly distinguishable from the pure perfect tense which ultimately ousted it from the language. A clear proof of this is found in those few passages where the apocopated form is employed; of these something will be said hereafter.[5] Another proof of this point is afforded by such idioms as the Arab. *lammâ ya'lam* 'he does not yet know'[6] and *'alam ta'lam* 'dost thou not know?'[7] in which the form of the verb can be explained only by reference to an analogous Accadian idiom. For example, the variant readings in *waraḫšu lā imlā-ma bienni elišu imtaqut* 'his month was not fulfilled and the *b.*-disease attacked him,' *i.e.* 'his (period of a) month was not fulfilled when the *b.*-disease attacked him,' and *waraḫšu lām imtalā binni elišu imtaqut* 'his (period of a) month (not yet=) before he fulfilled, the *b.*-disease attacked him,'[8] show that the Arab. *lam* 'not' and *lammâ* 'not yet' can be traced back through the Bab. *lām*(*a*) 'before' to its component elements *lā . . . -ma* 'not . . . indeed' or 'not . . . and.' That the Bab. *lām*(*a*) 'before' takes either the present or the preterite tense is immaterial to the argument; for its use with *iqṭul* suffices to show that the Arab. *lam*(*mâ*) 'not (yet)' as well as *'iḏ* 'when' and *'in* 'if' and similar words with *yaqtul* are governing not jussive forms but archaic preterite tenses, which have become stereo-

[1] Ex. *15*. 14.
[2] *Ibid*. 15.
[3] Jb. *3*. 3.
[4] Jer. *20*. 14.
[5] S. pp. 138–140.
[6] Qur'ân *Sûr*. *3*. 136.
[7] Wright, *Arab. Gramm.* II. 22 D; cp. Hebr. *hăṭerem tēḏa'* 'dost thou not yet know?' (Ex. *10*. 7).
[8] Ungnad, *Hamm. Ges.* II. *278*. 60–62.

X

Composite Languages in Palestine

The question at once arises whether any other evidence can be adduced in support of the theory that the syntax of the Hebrew verb represents two stratifications in the development of the language or rather two entirely different systems. For it may be argued that sporadic archaisms like those here cited from Arabic are one thing but that a completely duplicate system of tenses as that here postulated for Hebrew is a something very different. The answer is that the same phenomenon has repeated itself twice on Palestinian soil, and this agrees with the known facts of history in that country.

The records of the Old Testament directly attest the mixed origin of the Hebrew people, and these literary notices agree with the glimpses of their origin which can be gleaned from external history.[1] It is therefore natural to find that Hebrew contains elements derived from the various Semitic languages [2] and stereotyped not only in the vocabulary but also in the grammatical structure of the language.

That the Hebrew vocabulary is composite is apparent from the presence in it of numerous synonyms. For example, the four negative particles reflect different sources, inasmuch as the Hebr. *lō'* is identical with the Acc. *lā* and the Aram.-Arab. *lâ*, the Hebr. *'al* with the Acc. *ūl* and the Sab. *'l*,[3] the Hebr. *bal* with the Phœn. *bl*,[4] and the Hebr. *'î* with the Acc. *ai* or *ē* and the Eth. *ī-*; similarly, the Hebr. *'ēṯ* and *'im* 'with' correspond respectively with the Acc. *itti* and Phœn. *'t* and the Aram. *'im* and Syr. *'am*.[5]

The following table gives a list of common synonyms whose sources can be traced to the cognate language or languages from which they are drawn :—

(i) Synonyms of which one is found only in Hebrew (often including Phœnician and Moabite) :

Hebrew.		Accadian.	Aramaic.	Arabic.	Ethiopic.
bās	'trod down'	...	...	...	...
rāmas		...	*r*^{e}*mas*	*ramasa*	...

[1] S. pp. 151–152.

[2] Bauer (*Sprachmischung*, 17–20) cites a number of English and Scandinavian elements co-existing in the modern English language.

[3] Also Old-Aram. *'l* (possibly a Hebrew loan-word).

[4] Cp. Arab. *bal.* and Eth. *'enbala* 'without.'

[5] Cp. Sab. *'m* 'with.'

Hebrew.		Accadian.	Aramaic.	Arabic.	Ethiopic.
gā'al	'redeemed'	...	...	...	...
pāḏāh [1]		padū	...	faday	(fadaya)
ḥeres	'sun'	...	...	...	...
šemeš [2]		šamšu	šimšâ	šamšu	...
yāḇēš	'was dry'	...	yᵉḇēš	yabisa	yabsa
nāšat̲		...	...	...	...
'āśāh [3]	'did'	...	...	...	...
pā'al [4]		...	pᵉ'al	fa'ala	...
qāḏaḏ [4]	'bowed down'	qadādu	...	...	...
šāḥaḥ		...	...	...	...
śîm [2]	'to put'	šāmu	śîm	... [5]	šēma
śît̲ [2]		...	...	...	...

(ii) Synonyms of which both appear in the cognate languages:

Hebrew.		Accadian.	Aramaic.	Arabic.	Ethiopic.
'ēl [6]	'God'	ilu	...	...	...
'ĕlō'ᵃh		...	'ĕlāhâ	'ilāhu	...
bāzaz	'despoiled'	...	baz	bazza	...
šālal		šalālu	... [7]	...	...
ḥāzāh	'saw'	...	ḥăzâ	... [9]	...
rā'āh [8]		...	... [10]	ra'ay	re'eya
zāhāḇ	'gold'	...	dahăbâ	d̲ahabu	...
ḥārûṣ [6]		ḫurāṣu	...	...	...
yāhaḇ	'gave'	...	yᵉhaḇ	wahaba	wahaba
nāt̲an [2]		nad/tānu	... [11]	...	...
nᵉḇēlāh	'corpse'	nabultu	...	nabîlatu	...
peger		pagru	pagrâ	...	...

Occasionally two distinct roots drawn from different languages are used together as parts of the same word: such are *šāt̲āh* 'drank' from an Accadian and Aramaic and *hišqāh* 'gave to drink' from an Arabic and Ethiopic root. This too is a phenomenon found also in other languages. In inquiring into the sources of the language, however, caution must be taken to avoid what are or may be loan-words,[12] such as *'āzal*[13] for *hālak̲*[14] 'went.' It must also always be remembered that what seem to be synonyms from the few passages in which they occur may in reality not have had precisely the same sense. Yet it may be worth suggesting that a full investigation of the sources of the Hebrew vocabulary may possibly produce some illuminating results.

[1] Also Punic.
[2] Also Phœnician.
[3] Also Moabite.
[4] Also in Tall-al-'Amârna.
[5] Sab. *šm.*
[6] Also Phœnician.
[7] Syr. *šal(l)el*, probably a loan-word.
[8] Also Moabite.
[9] Arab. *ḥâzî* 'seer.'
[10] Aram. *rêwâ* 'appearance.'
[11] Syr. *net̲el* in the impf. tense.

[12] There are, of course, a few Sumerian loan-words in the Hebrew vocabulary, but they hardly enter into the present argument; such peculiar forms, however, as the Hebr. *šiḇ'āt̲ayim* 'sevenfold,' derived through the Can. *šibe/itān* from the Acc. *sibi* 'seven'+the Sum. TA.AM, which has a distributive force (Torczyner, *E.S.St.* I. 114, 179–180), are worth citing as illustrative of linguistic syncretism.

[13] Aram. *'ăzal* 'went'; cp. Arab. *'azalîyu* 'bygone.'

[14] Acc. *alāku* 'to go'; cp. Arab. *halaka* 'perished.'

Accadian.	Hebrew.	Phœnician.	Aramaic.	Syriac.	Arabic.	Ethiopic.
...	-ōh, -ô	...	-ēh	-eh	-ahu (-uh)	-hū, -ū, -ō
...	-mô	-m	...	...	...	...
Ass. anīni [1]	'ănaḥnû	'nḥn	'ănaḥnâ	...	...	...
Bab. nīni	naḥnû	nḥn	...	...	naḥnu (naḥnâ)	neḥna
attinā	'attēn(n)āh	...	...	...	'antunna	...
...	'attēn	...	'antēn	'a(n)teyn	...	'anten
...	hēm(m)āh	...	himmô	...	(hummâ)	...
...	hēm	...	...	...	hum	...
...	zeh	z	z	... [2]	...	ze
...	zû	...	...	...	[ḏû]	...
...	hazzeh (?) [3]	'z [4]	...	...	hāḏâ	...
...	hallāz	...	...	...	['allaḏ]	...
...	hallāzeh	...	...	...	['allaḏî]	...
...	zô, zôh [5]	z'	z', dâ	...	...	zā
...	zō'ṯ	zt	...	...	...	zātī
...	hazzōh(?) [3]	...	hāḏâ	hāḏeh	hāḏihi	...
...	hallēzû	...	...	...	['allatî]	...
...	'ēl	... [6]	'l	...	...	...
...	'ēlleh	...	...	...	'ûlâ, 'ûlā'i	'ellû
ša	šā-, še-	š-	...	...	...	...
...	zeh	...	zî	...	...	za
...	zû	...	...	...	(ḏû)	...
[ašar]	'ăšer	...	...	...	...	...
...	māh	m	mâ	...	mâ	...
...	mazzeh	...	...	...	māḏâ	...

The numerals, apart from the post-exilic *ʿaštēy ʿāśār*, which is borrowed from the Acc. *išteneširit* and replaces the pre-exilic *'aḥaḏ ʿāśār* corresponding with the Aram. *ḥaḏ ʿăšar* and the Arab. *'aḥada ʿasara*, exhibit only one proper instance of duplication; this lies in the fact that the fractions are formed on two models, those from one to nine being of the form *quṭl* and that derived from ten of the form *quṭṭāl*: thus *rōḇaʿ* corresponds with the Aram. *ruḇʿâ* and the Arab. *rubʿu*, while *ʿiśārôn* [7] belongs to the same scheme as the Acc. *šuššānu*, so that both the Accadian and the Aramæan-Arabic models find a place in the Hebrew scheme. Lastly, the strange *šiḇʿānāh* 'seven' as applied to Job's sons [8] may now probably be accepted as correct, since a text from Râs Šamrah has produced *šbʿny* 'Seventh' as the name of the seventh of the 'Gracious and Beautiful Gods,' [9] showing that a form in -(*ā*)*n*- beside the normal *šeḇaʿ* 'seven' is not impossible.

In verbs this duplication of forms runs through the whole

[1] Possibly an Aramaism (s. von Soden in *Z.A.* XL. 176[1]).

[2] Mand. *dh*.

[3] Josh. *2*. 17 and 2 Chron. *1*. 10 (s. G. R. Driver in *J.T.S.* XXX. 377–378).

[4] Pronounced *esse* or perhaps rather *asse* (Plautus).

[5] Judg. *16*. 28, where the masc. *hazzeh* is impossible with a fem. noun.

[6] Phœn. *'l* pronounced *ily* (Plautus), and so perhaps corresponding with Hebr. *'ēlleh* rather than *'ēl*.

[7] The Syr. *ʿušrâ* and the Arab. *ʿusru* show that a *qutl*- form would be expected; the Syr. *ʿešrônâ* is a Hebraism.

[8] Jb. *42*. 13.

[9] Virolleaud, in *Syr.* XIV. 132 (136), 64.

system, and is no less common in the regular than in the defective verbs, as the following table shows:

I. Strong verbs:

Accadian.	Hebrew.	Aramaic.	Syriac.	Arabic.	Ethiopic.
…	*zāḵart*	*dᵉḵert*	…	…	…
zakrāti	*zāḵartî*	…	…	*ḏakarti*	…
zakrū	*zāḵᵉrû*	*dᵉḵarû*	*dkar(w)*	*ḏakarû*	*zakarū*
…	*zāḵᵉrûn*	…	*dkarûn*	…	…
tazkurī	*tizkᵉrî*	…	…	…	*tezkerī*
…	*tizkᵉrîn*	*tiḏkᵉrîn*	…	*taḏkurîna*	…
izkurū	*yizkᵉrû*	…	…	…	*yezkerū*
…	*yizkᵉrûn*	*yiḏkᵉrûn*	…	*yaḏkurûna*	…
tazkurū	*tizkᵉrû*	…	…	…	*tezkerū*
…	*tizkᵉrûn*	*tiḏkᵉrûn*	…	*taḏkurûna*	…
…	*yizkōrnāh*	*yiḏkᵉrān*	…	…	…
…	*tizkōrnāh*	…	…	*taḏkurna*	…
…	*ziḵrî*	…	…	…	*zekerī*
zukrī	*zoḵrî* [1]	…	…	…	…
…	*zᵉḵôrî* [2]	*dᵉḵûrî*	*dkôrî*	*uḏkurî* (*ḏkûrî*)	…
nazkuru	*nizkōr* [3]	…	…	…	…
…	*hizzāḵôr* [3]	…	…	*inḏikâr*	…
zakkuru [4]	*zakkōr* [5]	*dakkôr(â)* [6]	…	…	*zakkerō* [7]
…	…	*dakkārâ* [6]	…	*ḏikkâr* [8]	…
…	*zakkēr*	*dakkēr* [6]	…	…	…
…	*yᵉhazkîr*	*yehaḏkir*	…	…	…
…	*yazkîr*	…	…	*yuḏkiru*	…

II. Weak verbs:

Accadian.	Hebrew.	Aramaic.	Syriac.	Arabic.	Ethiopic.
kapip	*kāp̱ap̱*	…	…	…	…
kap	*kap̱*	*kap̱*	…	…	…
…	*kāp̱ᵉpāh*	*kāp̱ᵉp̱aṯ*	…	…	…
kappat	*kappāh*	*kappaṯ*	…	*kaffat*	…
…	*kāp̱aptā*	…	…	*kafafta*	…
kappāta	*kappôṯā*	…	…	(*kaffêta*)	…
…	*yāḵōp̱*	…	…	*yakuffû*	…
…	*yikkōp̱*	*yikkōp̱*	…	…	…
…	*yāḵōppû*	…	…	*yakuffûna*	…
…	*yikkᵉpû*	*yikkᵉpû(n)*	…	…	…
kāpipu	*kōp̱ēp̱*	*kāp̱êp̱*	…	*kâfifu*	…
…	*kōʼēp̱* [9]	…	*kāʼep̱*	…	…
…	*yinṣôr*	*yinṭur*	…	*yanẓuru*	…
iṣṣur	*yiṣṣōr*	…	*neṭṭor*	…	…

---

[1] Ungnad (in *B.A.S.S.* V. 250) explains these imperative forms as coined on the analogy of the primitive *qutlū*.

[2] S. p. 32.

[3] Cp. Ahrens in *Z.D.M.G.* LXIV. 188–189 (s. Kautzsch & Cowley, *Hebr. Gramm.* 138²).

[4] Ass. *qarrubu*=Bab. *qurrubu* (Ylvisacker, *Z. b.-a. Gr.* § 34); cp. Can. *naṣur* for *naṣṣur*) beside *ḫalliq* (Böhl. *Spr. d. Amarnabr.* § 31 b).

[5] Only in four verbs (Kautzsch & Cowley, *Hebr. Gramm.* § 52 o).

[6] Levias, *Gr. of the Aram. Id., B.T.* 85–86.

[7] Cp. Barth, *Nb. S.S.* I. 154.

[8] Wright, *Arab. Gramm.* I. 115.

[9] Only in *šōʼsayiḵ* (Jer. *30*. 16).

Accadian.	Hebrew.	Aramaic.	Syriac.	Arabic.	Ethiopic.
ēqir	*yêqar*	*yêṭaḇ*	E. Syr. *neqar*	*yaibasu*	...
īqir	*yîqar*	...	W. Syr. *niqar*	(*yîbasu*)	...
...	*yiṣṣōr*	*yikkōl*	...	...	...
...	*yiṣṣaṯ*	*yiddaʿ*	...	...	...
...	*hauṣēʾ*	...	*ʾauʿī*	...	...
...	*hôṣēʾ*	*ʾôʿî*	...	...	...
...	*yeʾsōr*	...	...	*yaʾsiru*	*yeʾser*
...	*yōʾḵēl*	...	...	(*yôkul*)	...
muʾallidu	*meʾallēp̄*	...	...	*muʾallifu*	...
mullidu	*mallēp̄*	...	*mallep̄*	...	...
...	*raḇtā*	*qamt*	...	*qamta*	...
kīnāta	*rîḇôṯā*	...	...	...	...
...	*qāmîm*	*qāyemîn*	...	*qâʾimûna*	...
...	*qômîm*	...	...	...	...
...	*ḥāzû* [1]	...	...	...	*talawa*
...	*ḥāzāh*	*telâ*	*tlâ*	*talâ*	...
rami	[*ʿālāy*] [2]	...	...	*ramay*	*ramaya*
...	*ʿālāh*	*remâ*	*rmâ*	...	...
rabiat	*ḥāsāyāh*	*segîʾaṯ*	...	*saliyat* [3]	...
rabat	*ʿāśāṯ*	*reḇāṯ*	...	*salat* [4]	...
...	*rāḇeṯāh*	*benāṯâ* [5]	...	...	...
rabāta	*rāḇîṯā*	*reḇayṯā*, *reḇîṯ*(*ā*)	...	*salîta* [3]	...
...	*šālawtā*	...	...	*salawta* [4]	...
...	*ḥāsāyû*	...	...	...	*sarayû*
rabiū	*dāleyû*	*reḇîyû*	...	...	*ʿabeyū*
rabū	*rāḇû*	*reḇô*	...	*salû*,[3] *salau* [4]	...
izrū	*yeḥĕzû* [6]	...	...	*yaḏrû*	*yezarū*
...	*yeḥĕzeh*	*yiḥzê*	*neḥzeʾ*	...	...
tarbī	*tiznî* [7]	...	...	*taznî*	...
...	*tizneh*	*tiḇnēh*, *tiḇnēʾ*	...	...	...
...	*yišlāyû*	...	...	...	*yeʿbayū*
irbiū	*yirbeyûn*	...	...	...	*yesreyū*
irbū	*yirbû*(*n*)	*yirbôn*	...	*yislûna*,[3] *yislauna* [4]	...
bānītu	*hōmîyāh*	*dāmeyāh*	...	*sâliyatu*	...
bāntu	*hômāh*	...	...	...	...
...	*gallēh*	...	...	...	...
bunnū	*gallōh*	...	...	...	*fannewō*
...	*gallôṯ*	...	...	...	*fannewōt*

Hebrew accidence, then, is thoroughly mixed, and it is perhaps pertinent to ask whether the *-āh* in such idioms as the Hebr. *ʿênāyw qāmāh* 'his eyes were set,' [8] like the *-ā* in the Acc. *ḫummurā ēnātû*[*ni*] '[our] eyes are closed,' [9] is the feminine

[1] Only in Ps. *58*. 9, which means 'like the untimely birth of a woman (which) has not seen the sun' (for the subject of the verb cannot be the wicked, while the complex *nēp̄el ʾēšeṯ* is in the construct state governing the relative clause); cp. *ʿāśû* (Is. *2*. 20).

[2] As restored for M.T.'s *ʿălēy* in Jer. *8*. 18.

[3] From *saliya*.

[4] From *salâ*.

[5] Levias, *Gr. of the Aram. Id.*, *B.T.* 141.

[6] Only in Ps. *11*. 7, where the subject is not *penēymô*, as the Massoretes seem to have thought, but *yāšār*. Other examples are *yirʾû* 'he shall see' (Ps. *49*. 20), *yištaḥăwû* (Is. *2*. 8), 'he bowed down,' *wayešannô* (1 Sam. *21*. 14), and *wayyakkô* (2 Sam. *14*. 6), which ought probably to be vocalized respectively as *wayešannû* (for *wayešanneh*) 'and he changed' and *wayyakkû* (for *wayyakkeh*=*wayyak*) 'and he smote'; cp. Moab. *ʾʿn*(*n*)*w* 'I answered' and *wyʿn*(*n*)*w* 'and he answered.' Ought this ending to be pronounced *-ēw* or *-û*?

[7] Only in Jer. *3*. 6; cp. Pal. *arzi* (Knudtzon, *A.-T. 127*. 25)=Hebr. *ʾerṣeh*.

[8] 1 Sam. *4*. 15 (cp. Nöldeke, *B.S.S.* 19–20).

[9] Langdon, *Creation*, 84–85, i. 120.

plural ending or whether the singular verb is here collectively used; for arguments in favour of either view may be adduced. Thus, on the one hand, not only Accadian but also Biblical Aramaic and Ethiopic exhibit such a feminine plural ending; on the other hand, the collective construction, though not found apparently in Accadian, occurs in the tablets from Tall-al-ʿAmârna [1] and also in Biblical Hebrew, notably with the imperfect tense where the verb cannot be plural.[2] Again, Ethiopic and Aramaic use the plural verbs with collective nouns,[3] but in Arabic the collective construction is fully developed and widely used and in it even dual nouns may take feminine singular verbs.[4] In such a conflict of evidence it is perhaps impossible to reach a final decision.

Again, Hebrew shares certain peculiar verbal themes now with one and now with another language or group of languages. Thus it shares the *Pôʿēl* and *Kitpôʿēl* with Phœnician and Arabic, the *Nip̄ʿal* with Accadian as well as with Phœnician and Arabic, the *Nitpāʿēl* with Accadian, and the *Pᵉʿalʿal* with Ethiopic.

The striking thing about these comparisons is that Hebrew has far more duplicate forms than any other Semitic language, and the fact that tradition and history alike show the Hebrew people to have been of composite origin suggests that their speech may have been the same; if then this is so, these doublets are due not to the fact that the language went simultaneously through the same stages of development as the other Semitic languages in various countries and at various times but to the fact that they are derived from or are relics of all the dialects spoken by the diverse elements which have gone to mould the Hebrew people as known in history. There is therefore, for example, no need to condemn *tiznî* 'she plays the whore,' [5] or *ḥāzû* 'he saw' [6] and *yeḥĕzû* 'he sees' [7] as un-Hebraic and inexplicable even as Aramaisms; they are merely relics of the Accadian and Arabic (or rather proto-Arabic) elements [8] which are amongst the ingredients of the composite speech adopted and ultimately reduced by the Hebrews to a more or less homogeneous language and which lingered on beside the Hebræo-Aramaic *tizneh* and *yeḥĕzeh*, just as *zāḵart* and *zāḵartî*

[1] Cp. Brockelmann, *G.V.G.S.S.* II. § 103 c (where however the feminine plural nouns cited with feminine plural verbs are written ideographically).
[2] *E.g.* Ps. *37.* 31, *103.* 5 (s. Kautzsch & Cowley, *Hebr. Gramm.* § 145 k).
[3] Brockelmann, *G.V.G.S.S.* II. § 100 e. *a* and § 102 b. *a*.
[4] *Ibid.* II. § 99 f.
[5] Jer. *3.* 6 (s. p. 105); cp. Jer. *18.* 23, where *temḥî* stands for *timaḥ* (Neh. *13.* 14).
[6] Ps. *58.* 9 (s. p. 104).
[7] Ps. *11.* 7.
[8] Proper names as *ʿĂśîʾēl* (beside *ʿĂśāhʾēl*) and *Yaʿăśîʾēl* attest the persistence of such early forms down to a later period.

(which no one condemns as incorrect) continued to co-exist in use throughout the historic period.[1]

In the same way, the correspondence from Tall-al-ʿAmârna exhibits clear traces of two verbal systems drawn from distinct but cognate languages but so interwoven as to constitute a peculiar composite dialect. In it there exists side by side a double inflexion of *qaṭil* or *qaṭal* as the case may be, as seen in *naṣrāku* beside *naṣrāti* 'I protect(ed)' and in *gaštāku*[2] beside *kašadtu* 'I reach(ed)';[3] the same phenomenon, too, appears in the double inflexion of the preterite *iqṭul* or *ya/iqṭul*, as seen in *ikšud* 'he attained' beside *yikšudu* and *yakšudu* 'they attained.'[4] In each case the first example is Eastern, while the second is Western. It is further noticeable that there is the same twofold inflexion in the present *iqaṭal* or *ya/iqaṭal*,[5] although this tense is not otherwise found in Palestine; but its existence in these letters is an argument in favour of supposing it once to have existed in but to have been lost from Hebrew before the historic period.[6] What is, however, even more important for the present discussion is that this duplication is not confined to the inflexion of the tenses but extends to the meaning of the two forms which occur also in Hebrew. For in these same texts *qaṭi/al* covers the whole range of meanings possessed by the corresponding forms in Accadian and Hebrew, as in *šakin* 'it is' or 'may be put' beside *šakan* 'he has put,' *baliṭ* or *balaṭ* 'he is alive,' *kašadti* 'I have come' beside *kašdāku* 'I will come.'[7] So too *iqṭul* and *ya/iqṭul* exhibit the meanings both of the Accadian preterite *iqṭul* and of the Hebrew imperfect *yiqṭōl*: for example, in *imluk ištu libbiya* 'I decided in my heart,'[8] the vocalization of *imluk* is Western[9] while the preterite sense of

[1] Again, on the one hand such a form as the Hebr. *tāḇōʾṭāh* 'she comes' (Deut. *33*. 16; cp. Jb. *22*. 21), barbaric though it is, is not therefore impossible; for it is exactly illustrated by the equally barbaric Pal. *ibašat* 'she is' (Knudtzon, *A.–T*, *143*. 13), and *tašapparta* 'thou sendest' (*ibid*. *102*. 10). These hybrid forms, indeed, are not uncommon in the letters from Tall-al-ʿAmârna (s. Böhl, *Spr. d. Amarnabr.* 58–60), which proves them to have been current, at any rate dialectically, in Palestine at that time, and there need be no surprise if they lingered on as archaisms or dialectical peculiarities in classical Hebrew poetry; the only matter for surprise is that any have survived the levelling labours of the Massoretes. On the other hand, the peculiar Hebr. *yāḏeʿûn* (Deut. *8*. 3, 16) in the pure prose of the Deuteronomist may probably be dismissed as the work of an Aramaizing scribe, however this ending may be explained in Aramaic (s. Ungnad, in *B.A.S.S.* V. 237).

[2] For *kašdāku*.

[3] Böhl, *Spr. d. Amarnabr.* 45–48; Ebeling, in *B.A.S.S.* VIII. ii. 52–58.

[4] Ebeling, *ibid*. 45–46.

[5] Ebeling, *ibid*. 50–52.

[6] S. pp. 63–64.

[7] Ebeling, in *B.A.S.S.* VIII. ii. 52–58.

[8] Knudtzon, *A.-T*. *136*. 26–27.

[9] S. pp. 63–64; cp. Hebr. *ʾiqqāṭēl* beside *ʾeqqāṭēl* for *i* in place of *e* (Bauer & Leander, *Hist. Gr. d. hebr. Spr.* I. 319–320). This fluctuation in the vocalization helps to explain the confusion between the sing. 1st and 3rd persons in the Massoretic text.

the tense is of Eastern origin, while in *tišlaḫu ana yāši . . . u tinaizuni* 'they [1] do' or 'will flay (*i.e.* blame) me . . . and despise me,' [2] the Western imperfect *tišlaḫu* clearly has the same force as the Eastern present *tinaizu*; again, in *yīdi bēli inūma muḫḫišu amūtu* 'may my lord know that I will die for him' [3] and *ūl imât adi šû-ma šû* 'he will not die so long as he is is he (*i.e.* he remains as he is),' [4] the Western imperfect *amūt* (Hebr. *'āmûṯ*) and the Eastern present *imāt* (Ass. *imuat*, Bab. *imāt*; also *imuttu*) have almost the same sense.

That it is possible to demonstrate not only the existence of a twofold system in the syntax of the pre-Hebraic language of Palestine, but also that the accidence of the Hebrew language itself within the historic period exhibits clear traces of a composite origin,[5] is a strong argument in favour of accepting the theory here propounded that its verbal scheme too is derived from a twofold, an Eastern and a Western, source. At the same time it must not be supposed that forms and words here ascribed to such and such a language are derived from it either necessarily or directly. Many will, in fact, have descended from the common parent speech which lies behind all the Semitic languages, whence indeed all those which are shared by several of them will in all probability have come; others will have entered Hebrew through some other language, notably through Amorite, of which little can be said in default of direct evidence in the present state of knowledge; others again will be due to direct or indirect borrowing at a later rather than an earlier period in the development of the language. Yet, if indeed the mixed origin of the Hebrews is accepted, much will have been brought into their language by the various racial elements (Accadian, Amorite and proto-Arabic, Aramæan, Phœnician and Canaanite, and so on) which must have gone to the formation of the Hebrew race, and many of the peculiarities of Hebrew will be survivals from the diverse dialects of these peoples.

[1] *Sc.* the troops of the garrison, for which a feminine plural noun is used.
[2] Knudtzon, *A.-T. 137*. 12–14.
[3] *Ibid. 137*. 52.
[4] *Ibid. 20*. 69–70.
[5] S. p. 73.

XI

Force of Accadian Verbal Forms

The uses of the various verbal forms in Accadian, unlike that of those in Hebrew, is still far from being fully investigated and worked out, and it therefore seems advisable to set out briefly the view or views now generally held about them before making an attempt to compare them with those of the cognate languages.

Ungnad [1] explains the permansive as a perfect participle employed predicatively, mostly with a passive force like the Latin past participle; used actively with an object, it acquires almost the sense of the verb 'to have,' as in *mārī waldat* 'she has/had (borne and still) has/had sons' as distinguished from *mārī ūlid* 'she bore sons (at a definite moment in past time).' The present describes a momentary but still incomplete action, the preterite describes a momentary but completed action. Thus, on the one hand, 'the true verbal forms, the present and the preterite, originally designate momentary' or 'instantaneous action, the permansive, on the other hand, a lasting state,' [2] while 'in reference to present time it describes a lasting action.' [3] Bergsträsser,[4] depending on Landsberger, explains the distinction in meaning between these three forms as in the first instance purely objective, namely that they indicate a difference in the kind of action: 'the permansive is stative, the present describes durative activity, and the preterite has a momentary reference.' [5] Subsequently the present and preterite come to signify time, though predominantly in an objective sense; the *consecutio temporum* represents 'the order of the actions described by the verbs.' [6] The description of momentary actions employs *iqṭul* for the earlier and *iqtaṭal* for the later stages of the narration; in conditions the protasis uses *iqṭul* or *iqtaṭal* if there is one set or the one before the other if there are two sets of circumstances. Further, 'each stage or set can

[1] In *Bab.-ass. Gramm.* § 30.

[2] Germ. *Die eigentlichen Verbal-formen,* Præsens *und* Præteritum, *bezeichnen ursprünglich momentane Handlung, das* Permansiv *hingegen einen dauernden Zustand.*

[3] Germ. *Das præsentische* Permansiv *bezeichnet eine dauernde Handlung.*

[4] In *E.S.S.* 23.

[5] Germ. *Das* Permansiv *ist stativ, das* Præsens *fientischdurativ, das* Præteritum *punktuell.*

[6] Germ. *das Früher und Später der ausgesagten Handlungen.*

individually consist of several verbs in the same form.' [1] The expression of subjective time is only a secondary development; through it *iqṭul* acquires a past, *iqtaṭal* a momentary present, *iqaṭal* a durative present and future reference.

Deimel,[2] in discussing these two views, regards the permansive on the one hand as describing a permanent quality or peculiarity or a lasting condition; hence it is employed with stative verbs, such as 'to be great,' in which there is no consideration of time. Active verbs, too, have a form expressing a lasting condition, namely the perfect participle which, as in Latin, is normally passive. These verbs have the same force in the permansive also with an object and so correspond (as Ungnad says) in many ways with the verb 'to have' in European languages. The preterite and present-future on the other hand are reserved for verbs of action, but it must be borne in mind that verbs of state easily become verbs of action, as 'to be great,' easily passes into meaning 'to become great.' Active verbs, however, can have a threefold kind of action: 'momentary or instantaneous' [3] (*e.g.* 'to die'), 'iterative or punctuated' [4] (*e.g.* 'to tremble'), 'durative or drawn out' [5] (*e.g.* 'to run'). All three kinds of verb can occur in the preterite and present-future, but in the last two classes the kind of actions must be left out of consideration; for if it is desired expressly to designate lasting action, the present participle must be used.[6] The case of those few verbs, which by their nature refer to iterative action, is not so clear, but it seems that the *tan*- theme gives them iterative force, as a comparison of *illak* 'he goes' with *ittanallak* 'he goes to and fro' shows. If then a verb which by its nature describes durative action stands in the preterite, like *iṣṣur* 'he guarded,' this act can be called momentary or instantaneous only by disregarding the kind of action and taking the act by itself into consideration. If too 'he ran' is called a momentary action, the same must be said also of 'he runs' and 'he will run.' Further, it is self-evident that a verb which in itself refers to momentary action such as 'to die,' as distinct from 'to be dying,' cannot in the present-future (*e.g.* 'he dies, he will die') describe 'what is coming into being' or 'being done over a prolonged period

[1] Germ. *Jede Stufe kann ihrerseits aus mehreren Verben gleicher Form bestehen.*

[2] In *Orient.* III. 197–199.

[3] Germ. *momentane oder punktuelle.*

[4] Germ. *iterative oder punktierte.*

[5] Germ. *durative oder lineare.*

[6] The similarity of the permansive form to that of the present participle, however, makes it often difficult, if not impossible, to decide which is intended, but the purely verbal (predicative) use of the present participle seems to be very rare; even in such a case as *lû mulumminat egirrišu-ma* 'may she (be) a corrupter of' or 'corrupting his thoughts!' (Rawlinson, *C.I.W.A.* IV. 12 Rev. 36), the nominal origin of the construction is still perfectly clear; for the precative particle is used freely in purely nominal clauses.

of time '[1] (*e.g.* 'he is dying, he will be dying'). If the preterite of verbs expressing durative or drawn-out action is called instantaneous or momentary, this term naturally refers not to the kind of action described by the verbs in question but only to the subjective manner in which a kind of action in itself durative is interpreted;[2] the case of the Greek aorist may be cited as offering an analogous phenomenon. If then the same verbs stand in the present-future tense in reference to durative action, and this is described as 'what is coming into being' or 'being done over a prolonged period of time,' one is looking at the kind of action expressed by them. Thus the expressions 'momentary' or 'instantaneous' and 'coming into being' or 'being done over a prolonged period of time' do not stand on the same plane but rather result from two quite different points of view. With the same right and in the same sense as the preterite is called 'momentary' or 'instantaneous' is the present-future so called: according to the point of view, 'he ran' and 'he runs' are both momentary and both durative, but the one is complete and the other is incipient.

Finally, Deimel[3] has made a point in respect to the preterite which calls for remark. It is that in Accadian, when two verbs referring to past time follow one another in the preterite tense of the simple theme, the events described by them are synchronous, as in 'a man has married (*īḫuz*) a wife and has not drawn up (*iškun*) her marriage-contract,'[4] but that the *ta-* theme is used with the second verb as a future-perfect form if it refers to an event subsequent to that described by the first verb as in 'a man has married (*īḫuz*) a wife and a wasting disease has attacked her (*iṣṣabazzi*).'[5] As thus stated, the rule is hardly exact; for example, the context in 'a man has chosen (*iḫīr*) a bride for his son, and his son has had intercourse with her (*ilmazi*)'[6] shows that the first is regarded as preceding the second act in point of time, although both verbs stand in the simple theme, while the two acts are virtually synchronous in 'he has abandoned (*iddi*) his city and fled (*ittabit*),'[7] where the one verb is in the simple and the other in the *ta-* theme.[8] Further, a comparison of such passages as 'either a slave of the palace or a client's slave has married (*īḫuz*) a lady and she has borne (*ittalad*) him sons'[9] with 'a man has married (*īḫuz*) a wife

[1] Germ. *fientisch-durativ.*

[2] Germ. *nicht auf die Aktions-art der betr. Verba . . ., sondern nur auf die subjektive Art, wie man die an sich durative Aktionsart auffasst.*

[3] In *Orient.* III. 200.

[4] Ungnad, *Hamm. Ges.* II. *128.* 35–39.

[5] *Ibid. 148.* 65–69.

[6] *Ibid. 155.* 72–75.

[7] *Ibid. 136.* 57–59.

[8] Cp. *ibid. 162.* 78–81; *167.* 74–77.

[9] *Ibid. 175.* 57–63.

and she has borne him (*ūlizum*) sons (and) that woman has gone (*ittalak*) to her fate, (and) after her he has taken (*ītaḫaz*) another woman and she has borne (*ittalad*) sons '[1] suggests rather that, when a series of events occurring one after another is being narrated, the verbs describing the earlier stand in the simple and those describing the later stand in the *ta*- theme; and this makes it tempting to ask whether the purpose of the change of theme is not so much a wish to indicate the order of the events, which is sufficiently shown by the order in which they are set out, as a desire to avoid monotony by variety of form. Moreover, unlike the Babylonian code, the Assyrian laws show scarcely a trace of any such rule,[2] which confirms the suspicion that variety of theme is a matter of style rather than of meaning.[3]

[1] Ungnad, *Hamm. Ges.* II. *167*. 74–84.

[2] Cp. Driver & Miles, *Ass. L. 23*. 14–17, *36*. 85–88, *40*. 77–79 and 96–97 with *47*. 1–3 and 7–11.

[3] In this connection it may be remarked that the Assyrian laws show a marked tendency, if not to avoid the Ii theme, at any rate to prefer the Iii theme (*e.g.* Driver & Miles, *Ass. L. A. 12*. 14–19, *13*. 25–28, *B. 6*. 39–44).

This usage was easily extended to recurrent states or to actions repeated a definite number of times:

ACC. 'three times I was brought (*ṭuḫḫâku*) to the controller of the river.' [1]

The same form may then be employed to describe a single act or the state resulting from a single act in past time; in Accadian this idiom is not very common and is found chiefly in certain stereotyped phrases, in the other languages it occurs regularly when it is desired to describe an action in past time. Thus it may be used with aoristic force when the course of the narration fixes precisely the moment of the happening:

ACC. 'I was not detained (*kaliāku*) on account of the robbery, I was not caught (*kašdāku*) in the breach' [2]

HEBR. 'for with my staff I crossed over (*ʿāḇartî*) this Jordan'
'he became king (*mālaḵ*) in Jerusalem' [3]

ARAB. 'then his brother became king (*malaka*) after him.' [4]

Or as a pluperfect tense in cases where it is desired to bring two actions in past time into relation with each other and to indicate that the action thus described by the pluperfect tense took place before the other:

ACC. 'after they had made the division (*zîzu*), he again brought a claim' [5]

HEBR. 'thereon he rested from all the work which he had created (*bārâ*)'

ARAM. 'therefore Daniel went in unto Arioch, whom the king had appointed (*mannî*) to destroy the wise men of Babylon'

SYR. 'those whom one had led astray (*'aṭʿî*) he turned to the truth'

ARAB. 'he sat where his father had sat (*jalasa*)'

ETH. 'when he had spoken (*tanāgara*), he went out.'

Or as a perfect tense, when the speaker is not able to specify or is not desirous of specifying the exact time of the event:

ACC. 'he has been paid (*abil*), his heart has been gladdened (*ṭāb*)' [6]
'they have received (*maḫru*) the lead, the price of their field' [7]
'a scorpion has fallen (*maqut*) on a man' [8]
'I have not gotten (*ṣabtāku*) sense, I am not wise' [9]

[1] Ungnad, *B.B. 184*. 5–7.
[2] *Ibid. 154*. 31–32.
[3] *E.g.* 1 Ki. *14*. 21.
[4] Fleischer *Abulfed. Hist. Anteisl.* 84_{26}.
[5] Schorr, *U. Ab. Z.–Pr. 294*. 2.
[6] *Ibid. 279*. 31; *308*. 25.
[7] David & Ebeling, *A. Ru. 29*. 15–16.
[8] Meissner, *Stud. Ass. Lex.* II. 32_{22}.
[9] Rawlinson, *C.I.W.A.* IV. 19 *3*. 48.

HEBR. 'happy is the man who has found (*māṣâ*) wisdom'
ARAM. 'I have received (*qabbᵉleṯ*) thy letter.'

The state or action may have started in past and may continue into present time:

ACC. 'thou didst give me the slave and, since thou gavest (him to me), he has been ill (*maruṣ*)' [1]
'it is written down (*šaṭir*) so as not to be forgotten' [2]
'I have taken (*ṣabtāku*) the way and go quickly' [3]
HEBR. 'why is thine anger hot (*ḥārāh*), and why is thy face fallen (*nāp̄ᵉlû*)?'
ARAB. 'the commentators are agreed (*ittafaqa*)'
ETH. 'our sins are forgiven (*taḫadga*).'

In this way *qatil* or *qatal* came to be used with verbs denoting mental or spiritual states whose origin is past but whose effect is present:

ACC. 'as he wishes (*ṣibû*) [4]
'where he likes (*ḫašḫu*)' [5]
HEBR. 'I know (*yāḏaʿtî*) [6]
SYR. 'now I know (*yeḏʿeṯ*)'
ARAB. 'I wish (*šiʾtu*)'
ETH. 'I love (*ʾafqarkū*).'

It is also similarly used to describe a state or act which is only in course of being performed as the speaker speaks:

ACC. *endīku* [7] 'I stand'
HEBR. 'I lift up (*hărīmôṯî*) my hand'
SYR. 'our majesty commands (*peqdaṯ*)'
ARAB. 'I adjure (*ʿazamtu*) thee.'

Consequently it is used of states or actions which, having started in past and having continued into present time, have become habitual whether in the case of individual persons or in universal propositions:

ACC. 'the lusty god whose counsel is not changed (*enû*)' [8]
'the dead fear thee (*palḫuka*)' [9]
ARAM. 'a good vessel hides (*ks*[*h*]) a thing within it, but one which is broken leaks (*hnpqh*)' [10]

[1] Ungnad, *A.B.B. 94*. 22.
[2] Ebeling, *U.A.A.* 31, *V.A.T. 9329*, 8–9.
[3] Thompson, *Gilg.* 50. ix. (i) 7.
[4] Strassmaier, *B.T.*, *Cyr. 168*. 12.
[5] Chiera, *E.N.*, I. *101*. 11.
[6] Cp. Gk. οἶδα, Lat. *novi*.
[7] For *emdēku* (√ ʿ*md*).
[8] The present tense may be similarly used, as in 'by the exalted word of their divinity which is not changed (*inninnû*) his land thereafter rebelled against him' (Streck, *Assurb.* II. 82–83, x. 9–10).
[9] Ebeling, *Era.* 26–27$_8$. The Hebrew imperfect tense is similarly used, as in 'in Sheol who praises (*yôḏeh*) thee?' (Ps. *6*. 6, unless it has here a potential force).
[10] Cowley, *Aram. Pap.* 216, *ʾAḥ*, 109.

'let the word which I speak, when I speak, be acceptable (*lû magrat*)!'[1]
'let it not stick (*šakin*) in thy mind!'[2]

Aram. 'may he give (*ntn*) terror unto him!'[3]
'may his person be profaned (*'îṯhayyal*) as he profanes the week-days of the feast!'

Hebr. 'let all the nations be gathered (*niqbᵉṣû*) together and let there be assembled (*wᵉyēʼāsᵉpû*) the peoples'[4]
'do this unto them and let them live (*wᵉḥāyû*)'
'so let the Lord be (*wᵉhāyāh*) judge and give sentence (*wᵉšāpaṭ*) between me and thee, and let him see and plead my cause...'[5]

Syr. 'mayst thou be (*hwayṯ*) well!'

Arab. 'may his reign be lasting (*dâma*)!'
'may God not fill (*'asbaʿ*) thy belly!'

Eth. 'may I find (*rakabkū*) mercy!'.

Finally it may require the force of a command, though in Hebrew only with the permansive accentuation, where that is possible, and usually with the nominal consecutive *wāw*:

Ass. 'a hierodule whom a husband has married must be veiled (*paṣṣûnat*) in the streets'[6]
'thou must stay (*lū wašbāti*) ... until I come'[7]
'be not silent (*šuktumāt*); open thy lips'[8]

Hebr. 'go in ... and say (*wᵉʼāmartā*) unto him'[9]
'so love ye (*wa'ăhaḇtem*) the stranger'

Syr. 'go and be thou (*hwayt*) doing likewise.'

Second *yaqata/il*. This form was preserved only in the Accadian *iqaṭa/il* and the Ethiopic *yeqatel*; in both languages it was used to describe a state and preferably an act still unfulfilled, having a reference for the most part though not exclusively in Accadian to present or future and in Ethiopic to both times, so that it began by overlapping and finally ousted *qati/ul* and *qatal* from the field in this sphere.

[1] King, *Magic*, *8*. 15 (where Var. C. omits the precative particle).
[2] Knudtzon, *A.-T. 35*. 15.
[3] Cooke, *N.-S.I. 61*. 24. [4] Is. *43*. 9 (s. pp. 146–148). [5] 1 Sam. *24*. 16.
[6] Driver & Miles, *Ass.L. 41*. 61–62; the correlative clause in *41*. 62–65 has the present-future tense in 'one whom a husband has not married ... shall not be veiled (*tuptaṣṣan*).'
[7] Lutz *E.B.L. 117*. 7-8.
[8] This passage shows that *lā kalāta* in *alik lā kalāta* (Rawlinson, *C.I.W.A.* III. 15, *1*. 8) is not a circumstantial clause meaning 'without stopping' (Meissner, *K.A.G.* § 51, 1) but rather an instance of the permansive state used with imperative force in co-ordination with an imperative and meaning 'do not stop!' (M'Curdy, in *Actes du VIme. Congrès*, II. i. 521). Thus it is parallel in construction with *lā takallā* in *kuššid lā takallā* (Streck, *Assurb.* II. 326–327$_{18}$).
[9] Exod. 7. 26.

Thus it serves to describe states and acts incomplete and therefore continued or liable to be continued in past time:[1]

ACC. 'for six days and seven nights wind (and) deluge (and) storm was coming (*illak*) destroying (*isappan*) the land'[2]

ETH. 'continually I was sitting (*'enaber*) with you and teaching (*'emēher*).'

Such an act may be in present time, so long as it remains unfulfilled though continually repeated:

ACC. 'I cry (*adamum*) day and night'[3]

ETH. 'forgive us our sins as we forgive (*naḫadeg*) him who has sinned against us.'

Or it may be a single but unfulfilled act:

ACC. 'I am now sending (*ašappara*) my chief man'[4]

'why does not my lord agree (*imagur*)?'[5]

ETH. 'my speech seems (*yemasel*) false.'

It is therefore employed in universal propositions which describe what endlessly recurs and is ever present and so remains always incomplete:

ACC. 'the spawn of fishes fills (*umallā*) the sea'[6]

ETH. 'evil conversation corrupts (*yamasen*) good manners.'

It is also regularly applied to states and acts which are still future, since such are by their nature incomplete:

ACC. 'whatever I shall see (*ša āmaruni*), what I shall hear (*ša ašammūni*), I will declare (*aqabbi*) before my lord the king'[7]

'I shall send word (*ašappara*) to-morrow'[8]

ETH. 'the world which will come (*yemaṣe'*)'

'report what you shall hear (*tešame'ū*) and shall see (*terē'eyū*).'

In Accadian (but not in Ethiopic, where its place is taken by the subjunctive or jussive *yeqtel*) this form may also be

[1] Ungnad (*Bab.-ass. Gramm.* 39–40) sought to explain this usage as that of a historic present tense; but, as Bauer (in *B.A.S.S.* VIII. i. 21–22) remarks, the absence of such a construction in any historical narration, whether in verse or prose, militates against this view.

[2] Thompson, *Gilg.* 62–63, xi. 127–128.

[3] Zimmern, *Bab. Bussps.* 5. 59.

[4] Harper, *A.B.L.* III. *304*, Rev. 6–7.

[5] *Ibid.* IV. *382*. Obv. 8–9.

[6] Thompson, *Gilg.* 62. xi. 123.

[7] Harper, *A.B.L.* III. *317*. Obv. 8–10.

[8] *Ibid.* IV. *352*. Rev. 6–7, 12–13.

used by a natural extension of meaning in mild commands and prohibitions:

ACC. '(if) the tablet . . . turns up, it is false; it shall be destroyed (*iḫibi*)' [1]
'let him not take (*iṣabat*) his hand'
'thou shalt not be afraid (*tapallaḫ*).'

From these usages it will be seen how easily the same form came to be employed in circumstantial clauses describing states or acts which from the point of view of the subject of the main verb, whatever the time may be, are still unfulfilled:

ACC. 'I shrank back and sat weeping (*abakki*)' [2]
'he sits weeping (*ibakki*)' [3]
ETH. 'he saw an old man coming (*ya'atū*) from the field'
'I see him going (*yeḥawer*)'
'stay preaching (*tetnabāy*) to them.'

Third *yaqtul* (originally *yáqtul* but subsequently confused with *yaqtúl* and *yáqtulu*). As the tense of narration in past time this form was fully developed only in Accadian, in which no perfect tense was developed, while in those languages having such a tense it played a restricted and in fact a waning part; thus in Hebrew it survives as an independent tense accented after the western model almost exclusively in poetry, while in prose it is an archaism accented where possible like the Accadian preterite tense and marked by the verbal strong *wāw*, as also very probably in early Aramaic and certainly in Moabite, or by certain other particles; in Arabic, too, it is found only with certain definite particles.

It describes what is already complete in past time, primarily as an aorist in historical narration:

ACC. 'I fought (*amdaḫiṣ*) [4] with them, I brought about (*aškun*) their defeat' [5]
ARAM. 'and I lifted up (*w'ś'*) my hands to the lord of heaven, and there answered me (*wy'nny*) the lord of heaven' [6]
HEBR. 'but thou didst trust in thy beauty . . . and poured out thy whoredom on every one who passed by; his did it become (*yéhî*)' [7]

[1] Schorr, *U. Ab. Z.-Pr. 258.* 15–19 (where *iḫibi* stands for *iḫḫibi*). The perm. *ḫibi* is also commonly found in this phrase (*e.g., ibid. 237.* 1–4).

[2] The contrast between this and 'I sat and wept (*wā'ebkeh*),' where the state or act is regarded from the speaker's point of view as something completed in past time (Neh. *1.* 4), must be noticed.

[3] Thompson, *Gilg.* 66, xi. 290.

[4] For *amtaḫiṣ* (√ *mḫṣ*).

[5] Peiser in Schrader's, *K.B.* I. 100–101, iii. 36, 39.

[6] Pognon, *Inscr. Sém.*, 174 (*Zkr*), i. 11.

[7] Ezek. *16.* 15 (s. pp. 139–140).

'through the window the mother of Sisera looked forth and cried shrilly (*watt^eyabbēḇ*) through the lattice . . .; the wisest of her princesses answered her (*ta'anennāh*), yea she returned (*tāšîḇ*) answer to herself'

'then assembled (*'āz yaqhēl*) Solomon all the elders'[1]

MOAB. 'my father has been king over Moab thirty years and I have become king after my father; and I made (*w'ś*) this high-place for Chemosh'[2]

SAB. 'and when he raised his standard again and built (*wyjn'*) a siege-wall . . .'[3]

ARAB. 'he did not do (*lam yaf'al*) what they commanded him'[4]

'he has not presented himself (*lam yaḥḍur*).'

The event so described may be repeated a number of times:

ACC. 'twice seven times did I fall (*amqut*) at the feet of my lord'[5]

'yearly without ceasing he came to me (*illikam*)'[6]

HEBR. 'and they sent (*wayyišl^eḥû*) unto me after this sort four times and I answered them (*wā'āšîḇ*) after the same manner.'[7]

It may, however, serve also the purpose of a pluperfect tense; this happens in Accadian chiefly if not solely in dependent clauses and in Hebrew probably only with consecutive *wāw* in continuation of a perfect tense having pluperfect force:[8]

ACC. 'when I completed what I had built (*abnû*)'

HEBR. 'now Rachel had taken the teraphim and had put them (*watt^eśīmēm*) in the camel's furniture.'[9]

Fourth *yaqtúl* and *yáqtulu*. In Accadian and Ethiopic, which employed *yaqati/al* to describe incomplete states or acts, there is naturally no need of an imperfect *yaqtul(u)*; this, then, was evolved only in those languages in which *qatil* and especially *qatal* served as purely perfect tenses describing what is complete in past time, and there it served to make good the deficiencies of those forms, *i.e.* to describe what was incomplete without regard to the moment of the event or to its duration; thus it fulfilled functions entirely incompatible with those of the preterite *yáqtul*.

[1] 1 Ki. *8*. 1 (s. pp. 138–139).
[2] Cooke, *N.-S. I. 1*. 2–3.
[3] Kommel, *Süd-ar. Chrest.* 27–28 (where also Minæan examples are quoted).
[4] Qur'ân, *Sûr. 12*. 32.
[5] Knudtzon, *A.-T. 151*. 3.
[6] Thompson in *A.A.A.* XX. 87_{131}.
[7] Neh. *6*. 4.
[8] S. R. Driver, *Tenses*, 84–89.
[9] Smith, *B.H.T.* 84, ii. 8.

In past time it describes continuous or repeated states or acts :

HEBR. 'and the two of them were naked . . . and they were not ashamed (*yitbōšāšû*)'

'many times was he delivering them (*yaṣṣîlēm*), but they were rebellious (*yamrû*) in their counsel'

ARAM. 'I saw a dream, and it was terrifying me (*yᵉdaḥălinnanî*) and the thoughts upon my bed and the visions of my head were troubling me (*yᵉbahălunnanî*)'[1]

ARAB. 'one of them said : Verily I was seeing myself pressing (*'arânî 'aʿṣiru*) wine ; and the other said : Verily I was seeing myself carrying (*'arânî aḥmilu*) . . .'[2]

What is often repeated or continuous, however, may easily become habitual, so that the same form is used to describe what is wonted or customary :

HEBR. 'the sword of Saul used not to return (*tāšûb*) empty'

ARAB. 'I asked after the young men and where they used to assemble (*yajtamiʿûna*).'

Such habitual action, having begun in past time, may extend into present time and so be repeatedly fulfilling itself though remaining ever incomplete :

HEBR. 'therefore they eat (*yō'kᵉlû*) not the sinew of the hip . . . unto this day'

ARAM. 'according to the law of the Medes and Persians which passes not away (*teʿdâ*).'

Consequently this form is freely employed in gnomic sentences :

HEBR. 'a wise son gladdens (*yᵉśammaḥ*) his father'

ARAM. 'a sword troubles (*tdlḥ*) smooth waters[3] between good friends'[4]

ARAB. 'man arranges (*yudabbiru*) and God directs (*yuqaddiru*).'[5]

In present time this form describes what is happening at the moment and so is still incomplete :

HEBR. 'what are thou seeking (*tᵉbaqqēš*) ?'

[1] Kautzsch (*Gramm. d. Bibl.-Aram.* 136) is surely wrong in explaining these tenses as preterite.

[2] Brockelmann (*G.V.G.S.S.* II. § 78 *aa*) is surely wrong in explaining these tenses as preterite.

[3] *Angl.* 'stirs up bad blood' (s. G. R. Driver in *J.R.A.S.* LXIV. 88).

[4] Cowley, *Aram. Pap.* 216, *'Aḥ.* 113.

[5] Angl. 'man proposes but God disposes.'

ARAM. 'I have heard of thee, that thou art able (*tikkul*) to give interpretations and dissolve doubts'

ARAB. 'he only says to a thing, Be, and it is (*fayakûnu*)'
'what ails thee (that) thou art weeping (*tadmaʿîna*)?'

A form describing what is incomplete in past or present time can naturally be used in reference to future events; thus it is used regularly as a simple future tense:

HEBR. 'we shall surely die (*nāmû̱t*), because we have seen God'

ARAM. 'after thee shall arise (*tᵉqûm*) another kingdom'

ARAB. 'so God shall judge (*yaḥkumu*) between them at the day of resurrection.'

Then from describing what is merely future in time, it passes by an easy transition into serving in wishes or intentions and mild commands, when it may be and often is indistinguishable from the jussive *yaqtul* both in form and in meaning:

HEBR. 'nay, I will die (*'āmû̱t*) here'
'he shall surely be put to death (*yûmā̱t*)'

ARAM. 'when it is time, we will divide (*nplg*) them between us'[1]

ARAB. 'you shall depart (*tanṣarifûna*), and we will consider (*nar'ay*) the matter between us.'

Finally, inasmuch as it describes what is incomplete, it was sometimes employed in circumstantial clauses; in this construction in Hebrew it was largely ousted by the participle, while in Arabic it for the most part gave way to a special use of the accusative case:

HEBR. 'shall anyone teach God knowledge when judging (*yišpôṭ*) those on high?'
'behold! my father does nothing either great or small without informing (*yiḡleh*) me'
'I laughed at them not having confidence (*ya'ămînû*)'

SYR. 'he leaves me feeling ashamed (*'eḇhaṯ*)'

ARAB. 'and they came to their father in the evening, weeping (*yabkûna*).'

Fifth *yaqtul*. As already said, the jussive *yaqtul* was in origin unconnected with the preterite *yaqtul* and the imperfect *yaqtul(u)*, being a new formation intended to make good the deficiencies of the imperative *qutul*.[2] Its force was cohortative, voluntative, precative, jussive; and, being in many cases in form indistinguishable from or confused with

[1] Cowley, *Aram. Pap. 28*. 13–14. [2] S. pp. 33–35.

the preterite and imperfect tenses, it was often accompanied by a special particle or termination indicative of the required sense:

ACC. ‘let him hear (*lišme*) my precious words’ [1]
‘come! let us go (*ī nīlika*)’ [2]
‘mayst thou not have (*tarši*) a rival!’ [3]
‘let it not return (*itūr*) to its place!’ [4]
‘where am I to go (*lullik*)?’ [5]
‘let my lord hear (*yišme*) my words!’ [6]
ARAM. ‘may he eat (*l'kl*) in distress!’ [7]
‘whatever he asks let him not give (*ytn*) him!’ [8]
‘may there be (*yhwy*) peace upon thee!’ [9]
HEBR. ‘let there be (*yᵉhî*) light!’
‘let there, pray, not be (*tᵉhî*) strife!’
ARAB. ‘may there be (*yakun*) a share in good deeds from thee!’
‘may thy Lord make an end (*liyaqḏi*) of us!’
‘be not grieved (*taḥzin*)!’
ETH. ‘may the Lord preserve thee (*yeʿqabeka*)!’
‘let there be (*layekūn*) light’
‘do not kill (*teqtelū*) him.’

These few examples will have served their purpose if they have sufficed to show that every phenomenon of Hebrew usage finds a parallel idiom in one or other of the Semitic languages; and the fact that it seems to incline now to the one and now to the other side confirms the suspicion that the syntax is not homogeneous but, like the accidence, composite in origin. Consequently, all attempts to explain it as a uniform system must be abandoned in favour of one based on the recognition of its historical development. Only so will the many irregularities postulated by the current explanations disappear as they find their place as integral elements of Semitic and therefore of Hebrew speech.

1 Ungnad, *Hamm. Ges.* II. xxv. b. 12–14.
2 Ebeling, *Fabel*, 10, R. 5.
3 Jensen in Schrader's *K.B.* VI. i. 48–49$_{38}$.
4 Langdon, *B.P.P.* 24, K. 2999$_{13}$.
5 Thompson, *Gilg.* 65, xi. 230.
6 Knudtzon, *A.-T.* *107*. 25; cp. *105*. 83.
7 Cooke, *N.-S. I.* *61*. 23.
8 *Ibid.* 22–23.
9 Cowley, *Aram. Pap.* 216, 'Aḥ. 110.

XIII

Accadian and Hebrew Idioms

In Accadian the relationship of the permansive *qaṭil* to the present *iqaṭal* on the one side and to the preterite *iqṭul* on the other side and of these two tenses to one another requires clear definition, so far as that is possible, and a few examples may here be set out and examined with that object in view, especially as some uses come rather close to idioms commonly found in Hebrew.

The permansive state is distinguished from both tenses by the fact that it always describes a more or less lasting condition. Thus, for example, in

> 'since thou didst leave [me] (*tēziban*[*ni*]) I have been' or 'was ill (*marṣāku*); I did not put (*aškun*) my foot to the ground'[1]

as also in

> 'the Aramean(s) were hostile and (*nakir-ma*) took (*iṣbat*) the entrance to the ford'[2]

and

> 'a task have I undertaken and (*ṣabtāku-ma*) did send (word) (*ašpura*) to my brother'[3]

and

> 'over against . . . they drew up the line of battle, the approach to my watering-place they occupied and (*ṣabtu-ma*) sharpened (*uša'ilu*) their weapons'[4]

the permansive forms describe a more or less lasting state, while the preterite tenses define a single act in past time. Particularly in the first passage *aškun* derives point from the fact that the tense implies a momentary act. In the second the attachment of the permansive state by means of *-ma* to the preterite tense exactly reflects the Hebrew use of strong *wāw* connecting a perfect with a following imperfect tense; and

[1] Ungnad, *Ab.B. 123*. 1–3.
[2] King, *Chronicles*, II. 81_{7-8}; cp. Thureau–Dangin, in *R.A.* XXI. 50, *68*. 5–9.
[3] Knudtzon, *A.-T. 7*. 63.
[4] Bezold in Schrader's *K.B.*, 106–107, v. 47–49 (s. Meissner in O.L$_2$. XIX. 306 .

indeed, although the Accadian *qaṭil* and the Hebrew *qāṭal* have different shades of meaning, the comparison shows that the Hebrew construction is explicable without resort to the doctrine of nascence or emergence if the Hebrew *yiqṭōl* is in such idioms equated with the Accadian *iqṭul*. Inversely, a preterite tense may be joined to a following permansive state by means of the same enclitic particle as in

'the way to Accad their forces took and (*iṣbatunim-ma*) were come (*tebūni*) to Babylon '[1]

where the preterite *iṣbatunim* describes the start of the journey or perhaps the journey itself viewed as a single act in contrast with the arrival in which it terminated and which became more or less a permanent state. A similar passage is

'I received (*elgi*)[2] the 40 shekels of silver . . . and have been paid (*u aplāku*),'[3]

where the meaning of the tenses is the same but the conjunction *u* is preferred to the particle *-ma* owing to the influence of the permansive state.[4] This then illustrates the use of *û-* instead of *wa-* when joining a consecutive perfect to a preceding imperfect tense, though in a different time-sphere.

Again, in such a passage as

'the chariots together with their mares, whose riders indeed . . . had been slain (*dīkû*) and who had been let loose (*muššurā*) and were going to and fro (*ittanallakā*) by themselves, I straightway brought back (*utirra*)'[5]

the permansive *dīkû* and *muššurā* define a lasting state, the present *ittanallakā* describes a continuing activity in past time, and the preterite *utirra* describes a single act putting an end to the scene[6]. So too in

'I despatched (*uma'ir*) my horse-chariots after them to pursue them; with their weapons they were striking down (*urasapu*) their fugitives who had gone forth (*ūṣû*) for their lives, wherever they were arriving (*ikaššadu*)'[7]

the tenses are the same, except that in place of the permansive

[1] Bezold in Schrader's *K.B.* 106-107, v. 39–40. [2] For *elqi* (√ *lqḫ*).

[3] Chiera, *E.N.* I. *25*. 7–10; cp. Pfeiffer *E.N.* II. *103*. 28–32, *108*. 28–31.

[4] Normally *u* is used with the permansive state, but *-ma* may be employed to connect it with a verbal form (s. pp. 91–94).

[5] Bezold in Schrader's *K.B.* II. 110–111, vi. 9–13. This passage offers clear examples of the distinction between the masc. plur. *-u* (in *dīkû*) and the fem. plur. *-ā* (in *muššurā* and *ittanallakā*) and the ventive *-a* (in *utirra*).

[6] S. pp. 108–110. [7] Bezold in Schrader's, *K.B.* II. 110–111, vi. 21–24.

state with a pluperfect force the preterite *ūṣû* is used as action is contemplated.

The distinction between the imperfect *iqaṭal* and the preterite *iqṭul* is clear: the former describes what is incomplete, whether past or present or future, and ought to be called not the present or future but the imperfect; the latter describes what is past and not continuing and ought to be called the preterite or aorist tense. Thus in

> 'the dove went (*illik*) but returned (*itūram*); there was (*ipaššum*)[1] no resting-place and it turned back (*iṣṣaḫra*)'[2]

the three verbs in the preterite tense describe single acts, while the present *ipaššum* describes the state of no resting-place which was then continuous. Such, too, is the distinction between these same two tenses in

> 'Tiamat indeed cried (*issi*) aloud in a rage
> 'her limbs altogether shook (*itrurā*) to (their) foundation'[3]

and

> 'the goddess Ishtar was crying (*isišsi*) like a woman in travail';[4]

the preterites *issi* and *itrurā* describe the single loud cry of rage and the momentary quivering of her limbs which interrupted her chant, the imperfect *isišsi* describes the prolonged crying aloud of one in continuous pain, as Bauer has explained it.[5] So, when the two tenses stand together, as in

> 'death did I fear (*aplaḫ*) and was ranging (*arappud*) the desert'

the fear is depicted as a single act by contrast with the continuous ranging over the desert of which it was the cause and which lasted a considerable length of time.[6]

Two other passages, where the variation of the tenses is singularly instructive, may also be compared. First, in

> 'When heaven above was not named (*nabû*),
> '(and) earth beneath was not called (*zakrat*) by name,
> 'Apsū indeed the primeval, their sire,
> 'Mummu (and) Tiamat who brought them all to birth
> 'mingled (*iḫīqu*) their waters together:

[1] For *ibašši-ma*.
[2] Thompson, *Gilg.* 63, xi. 147–148; cp. 150–151.
[3] Langdon, *Creation*, 138–139, iv. 89–90.
[4] Thompson, *Gilg.* 62, xi. 116 (s. p. 128).
[5] In *B.A.S.S.* VIII. i. 22².
[6] Thompson, *Gilg.* 50, ix. (i) 5.

'but dark chambers were not constructed (*kiṣṣurā*), marsh-lands were not seen (*še'ā*),
'when none of the gods had been brought forth (*šūpû*)
'(and) were not called (*zukkuru*) by name (and) fates were not fixed (*šīmu*);
'then were the gods created (*ibbanû*) in their midst,'[1]

a series of verbs in the permansive state describes the primeval condition of the world, but the description is twice interrupted: on the first occasion a sudden change is introduced by the preterite *iḫīqu* which depicts a momentary act in contrast to the nameless state of the universe existing from all eternity (while there occurs as an interesting variant reading in one version the present *iḫiqqu* which depicts the change as something not immediately fulfilled but continuing for some time); on the second occasion the description is broken off to describe the creation of the gods where unfortunately the ambiguous *ibbanû*, probably intended as a preterite tense, is used. Second, in the legend of the flood it is recounted in the text how

'brother was not seeing (*immar*) brother,
'people were not being espied (*utaddā*)[2] from the heavens;
'the gods did fear (*iplaḫu*) the storm and
'shrank back (*itteiḫsu*),[3] they ascended (*ītelû*) to the sky-god's heaven;
'the gods like a hound were crouching (*kunnunu*), they were lying (*rabṣu*) in distress (?);
'Ishtar was crying (*isišsi*)[4] like a woman in travail,
'the fair-voiced Lady of the gods was howling aloud (*unambā*)'[5]

here the present tenses depict continuous activity or effort, the preterite tenses describe single acts, and the permansive forms refer to continuous states regarded as conditions of inactivity; the only other point worth comment is the preterite *iplaḫu*, which expresses not so much a state of fear as an act of panic.

[1] Langdon, *Creation*, 66–67, i. 1–9. Burney (in *J.T.S.* XX. 208–209), seeking to support the theory of nascent or emergent action by tracing it back from Hebrew into Accadian, suggests that, while the permansives—*nabû, zakrat, šūpû, zukkuru, šīmu*—describe states, the preterites—*iḫīqu, ibbanû*—describe nascent or emergent actions, *i.e.* that *iḫīqu* means 'they went on to mingle' and *ibbanû* means 'they came to be created.' Such an idea, however, is contrary to the whole usage of the Accadian preterite tense in countless passages, and there is no need to go beyond the simple idea that, while the permansive describes an enduring state, the preterites are contrasted with them as describing single and virtually instantaneous or momentary acts in past time.

[2] Probably, like the parallel *immar*, in the present tense.

[3] Probably, like the parallel *iplaḫu*, in the preterite tense.

[4] S. p. 127.

[5] Thompson, *Gilg.* 62, xi. 111–117.

In Hebrew difficulty arises in the use of the perfect tense in a number of passages which resemble those here discussed and where it is introduced by weak *wāw* in reference to past time.[1] Such a passage is

'and he was believing (*wᵉhe'emīn*) in Yahweh, and he counted it (*wayyaḥšᵉḇeāh*) to him for righteousness,' [2]

where the Hebrew perfect tense clearly describes a more or less lasting state, *i.e.* it marks Abraham's belief as a continuous state, in contrast with the definite act whereby it was reckoned to him for righteousness.[3] Similarly the Accadian permansive state is frequently preferred to the preterite tense in verbs of trusting and fearing and such like, as in

'the people dwelling therein in their steep mountains were trusting and (*taklu-ma*) were not fearing (*pitluḫu*) the lordship of Ashshur,' [4]

where the state thus described is depicted as lasting; and with this must be contrasted the preterite tense in

'in the help of one another they trusted and (*itaklu-ma*) joined (*ikṣuru*) battle,' [5]

where the reference is to a definite event in past time. In Accadian, then, the choice of any given part of the verb depends not merely on the nature of the happening which it is desired to describe, *i.e.* whether it is incomplete or complete, but also at any rate to some extent on the point of view from which it is regarded, *i.e.* whether it is viewed as a state or an act; and it may be surmised that the same practice may have been extended also to Hebrew.[6] Yet it must be admitted that by no means all the passages where the perfect tense with weak *wāw* takes or seems to take the place of the imperfect tense with strong *wāw* can be explained; some may be due to the increasing tendency to give up the archaistic construction with consecutive *wāw*, some to the love of variety or unskilful writing, while others may even be due to textual corruption.

In the letters from Tall-al-ʿAmârna Böhl [7] has drawn attention to several passages in which it is difficult at first sight

[1] S. R. Driver, *Tenses*, § 133. [2] Gen. *15*. 6 (E).

[3] Cp. Gen. *34*. 5 (JE) for similar uses of the perfect tense with weak *wāw* in reference to lasting states (s. p. 113).

[4] Streck, *Assurb*. II. 166–167, Rev. 7–8.

[5] Peiser in Schrader, *K.B.* I. 158–159, i. 43–44.

[6] Something similar is already recognized in the extended use of the perfect tense in a present sense with stative and certain allied verbs (S. R. Driver, *Tenses*, § 11).

[7] In *Spr. d. Amarnbr*. 79.

to explain the use of the present-future (or present, as he calls it) tense if it describes what is incomplete; it seems rather as though the preterite *iqṭul* ought to have been used, but the present *iqaṭa/il* has perhaps been chosen for the sake of vividness in depicting past events in historical narrative. In this connection the following eight passages [1] call for remark. In

> 'formerly my father was sending to thee (*išapparakum*) a messenger and thou wast not detaining him (*takallāšu*) many days; quickly wast thou letting him come (*tukašadaššu*) and thou didst have a good gift conveyed (*tušeibbilam*) to my father' [2]

the first three verbs in the present tense describe the prolonged and perhaps repeated process of sending an envoy, while the fourth verb in the preterite tense describes the single act with which the business was concluded. In

> 'See! thy father is' or 'was not come forth (*azi*) [and] is' or 'was not seeing (*idagal*) the lands' [3]

the present *idagal* merely describes what, regarded from the standpoint of the permansive *azi*, is still unfulfilled, whether the scene is regarded as past or present. A similar explanation is possible in the case of

> 'I sent word (*šaprāti*) . . . when Amanappa was coming (*yīla[kuna]*) with a small force and I did send' or 'was sending word (*aštapar*) [4] to the palace and the king was sending (*yuwašara*) . . . a large force; (but) Abdi-ashirta together with all his property was not taken (*laki*),' [5]

where the permansive *šaprāti* is used with aoristic force because the course of the narrative fixes the precise moment of the happening, *i.e.* when Amanappa was coming; a series of successive events is then vividly described by a succession of verbs in the present tense as occurring in such rapid succession as almost to overlap one another, and the whole series results in a state described by the permansive *laki*. In

> 'and lo! his son was plundering (*yiḫa[bat]*) Zumur' [6]

[1] The two cases of *iṣṣabat* are omitted, as the verb may be explained as in the preterite tense (Knudtzon, *A.-T. 75*. 30–31 and 35–36).

[2] Knudtzon, *A.-T. 3*. 9–12.

[3] *Ibid. 116*. 61–62.

[4] The tense in the Iii theme is ambiguous.

[5] Knudtzon, *A.-T. 117*. 21–28.

[6] *Ibid. 131*. 37–38.

the exclamatory particle shows that the event is regarded vividly as coinciding with those just described. In

'my lord, I was dwelling (*ašpāku*) in Tunip and did not know (*īte*) that he was come (*gašid*); so soon as I was hearing (*išeimmi*), then I went up' or 'was going up (*eteilli*) [1] after him, but was not overtaking him (*agašadšu*)' [2]

the tenses explain themselves: the permansive states describe the circumstances of the case, while the present tenses again describe vividly what the writer was doing so soon as he was learning the news; the whole episode is depicted as a state of continuous activity, intended without doubt to convey a sense of occupation and efficiency to the reader, who of course was none other than the king. The mixture of tenses in

'the SA-GAZ have taken (*ṣabtu*) and were plundering (*išalalu*) Mahzibti . . . and did set it (*ušširuši*) on fire,' [3]

is curious, but the present *išalalu* may perhaps be explained as due to a desire to distinguish the prolonged business of plundering the city from the brief, almost momentary, operations of setting it on fire. Somewhat differently in

'and my brothers said to Amanhatbi: Give up the SA-GAZ the enemies of our lord the king . . . ; and he was consenting (*imagar*) to give up the SA-GAZ, but he took them (*ilkišunu*) . . . and fled (*innabit*) to the SA-GAZ' [4]

the present *imagar* describes a process contemplated and perhaps begun but obviously never completed. Lastly, the force of the tense is purely present in

'my lord, the king of the Hatte is coming (*îllagam*) into the land of Nuhashshe and I cannot (*ili'e*) come,' [5]

since the writer is clearly describing an event going on but still incomplete at the moment of writing.

Clearly, then, in all these passages a case can be made out for a vivid use, especially since a deictic particle is sometimes added to the present-future tense of incomplete action. It ought, however, to be remembered that none of the writers are persons whose native language is Babylonian and indeed that only one of them is a Semite, and that an Aramæan; consequently there is no reason to expect a correct or consistent use of the tenses in their correspondence.

[1] The tense in the Iii theme is ambiguous.
[2] Knudtzon, *A.-T. 161*. 12–16.
[3] *Ibid. 185*. 16–19.
[4] *Ibid. 185*. 54–63.
[5] *Ibid. 164*. 21–23.

XIV

Hebrew Preterite Tense

Birkeland [1] has examined a number of passages in the Old Testament where the consecutive *wayyiqṭōl* occurs with a view to showing that it is properly a preterite tense; for he holds that, while the diverging forms of the verb with so-called consecutive *wāw* represent an older stage of the language than those of the plain imperfect, there is naturally a connection between the two forms, but that this fact must be explained rather as a matter of linguistic history than as arising out of their actual use in Hebrew. Although, too, the consecutive form is always attached to something preceding, it is by no means evident that it is timeless as the preceding forms may be. This is especially noticeable when it is attached to a relative clause expressed by means of a participle, which is in itself timeless, or to an equally timeless infinitive construction, as in

> 'who then is he that hunted venison and did bring (*wayyāḇē'*) it me?' [2]

and

> 'as I lifted up my voice and did cry (*wā'eqrā'*).' [3]

The most significant fact, however, is that in the whole narration of events from 'Genesis' to 'Kings' there is scarcely a consecutive imperfect tense in which the preterite sense is not manifest, whereas both the perfect and imperfect forms are used for every kind of time throughout these books.

The preterite usage may not be denied even where a modern language employs a perfect or pluperfect tense; thus the Hebrew preterite is nearer to the English tense in 'I have been here for a long time' than to the German tense in *ich bin hier schon lange Zeit*, as in

> 'and Joshua set up twelve stones . . . and they are' (as in the R.V.) or 'have been (*wayyihyû*) there unto this day.' [4]

There are abundant examples of this idiom which, rightly

[1] In *Act. Orient.* XIII. 5–30.
[2] Gen. *27.* 33; cp. Dan. *8.* 22.
[3] Gen. *39.* 18; cp. *28.* 6.
[4] Josh. *4.* 9.

explained, in every case refers to an event already begun or already past from the speaker's point of view,[1] although this may not be immediately apparent, as in

'and it was told Joab, Behold! the king was weeping and did mourn (*wayyiṯ'abbēl*),[2]

where the past tense refers to the king's behaviour at the moment when the *ex hypothesi* messenger who brought the news left David, and in

'and they said, This fellow came in to sojourn and did judge (*wayyišpōṭ*),'[3]

where the sense is that the man had already, before their speaking, acted as judge.

In the prophets there is no proof of a present usage of the consecutive construction, but the consecutive imperfect tense has a preterite force, especially when it immediately precedes a verdict or sentence of condemnation[4]; for either it refers to events actually past or the action which is the subject of the verdict must already have begun at the moment when they are speaking. Examples are

'because ye despised this word and did trust (*wattiḇṭaḥû*) in oppression and perverseness . . .,

'therefore this iniquity to you shall be as a breach ready to fall,'[5]

where a translation in the present tense (as in the R.V.) is contrary to the spirit of the text.

The same usage is found commonly in hymns extolling the doings of Yahweh, as in

'he rebuked the sea and did make it dry (*wayyabbᵉšēhû*) and all the rivers he parched up,'[6]

where the allusion must be to some such particular event as the crossing of the Red Sea, although the poet has generalized it by speaking of plural rivers; moreover, what Yahweh has once done he can do again, but this does not justify the

[1] *E.g.* Gen. *31*. 15, *32*. 5; Exod. *4*. 23; Numb. *22*. 11; 1 Sam. *2*. 29; 2 Sam. *3*. 8; 1 Ki. *19*. 10.

[2] 2 Sam. *19*. 2 (where the Targum's participle is a paraphrase due to a misunderstanding of the idiom); cp. 1 Ki. *8*. 7 (where the historian is describing something not existing in his time).

[3] Gen. *19*. 9 (where the R.V.'s 'and he will needs be a judge' is an impossible translation).

[4] Cp. Is. *50*. 7, where *wā'ēḏa' kî lō' 'ēḇôš* means either 'and I knew that I should' or 'and I (have come to) know that I shall not be ashamed.'

[5] Is. *30*. 12; cp. Jer. *6*. 14, where the verdict begins in the middle of the following verse.

[6] Nah. *1*. 4; cp. Ps. *33*. 9.

translation of the preterite, which introduces a concrete fact as evidence of the general assertion of Yahweh's ability, as a present tense, as though the miraculous drying up of the rivers is a habitual activity of Yahweh. So, too, in

'the voice of Yahweh breaks the cedars,
'and Yahweh did break (*wayᵉšabbēr*) the cedars of Lebanon,' [1]

the participle is general while the preterite tense describes a particular event, as its localization on Lebanon shows, is proof of the preceding assertion. Only in some such way, too, is it possible to account for the difficult tense in

'the Lord killeth and maketh alive, he bringeth down to Sheol and did bring up (*wayyaʿal*); [2]

here the point is that the participle describing how Yahweh brings men down to Sheol refers to the general truth that all men descend there in the fulness of time, while the preterite *wayyaʿal* refers to some unique and particular event in history.[3] In other instances the reference is to indefinite events in the history of the nation or of individual persons, where too the general picture is reinforced by particular examples, as in

'the angel of the Lord encamped round about them that feared him and did save them (*wayᵉḥallᵉṣēm*),[4]

where the argument is that the Psalmist was able to call confidently on the Lord because His angel is ever encamped around those who fear Him and His power is known because He saved them in past times.

As in hymns predicating various attributes of Yahweh, so in psalms of thanksgiving passages commonly cited in favour of a timeless use of the consecutive imperfect tense can also be explained on the assumption that it really has a preterite sense. For example, in

'and as for me, thou didst uphold me in mine integrity, and didst set me (*wattaṣṣîḇēnî*) before thy face for ever' [5]

the Psalmist declares his certainty that Yahweh delights in him because on some definite occasion He has supported him and taken notice of him; the reference is to an individual act

[1] Ps. *29*. 5; cp. Is. *40*. 22, where the reference is to the creation of the world.
[2] 1 Sam. *2*. 6.
[3] Cp. Am. *5*. 8, where the perfect *heḥĕšîḵ* is parallel with the preterite *wayyišpᵉḵēm*, and the two verbs may refer 'to some destructive inundation' as a historical occurrence (s. Edghill, *Amos*, 51).
[4] Ps. *34*. 8.
[5] Ps. *41*. 13; cp. *92*. 8, 11, 12.

of salvation, and it is therefore incorrect to assign a present sense to the preterite tense. Indeed, the picture loses force by being deprived of its application to the fortunes of the individual Psalmist and being interpreted as a vaguely generalizing observation on life. Such an explanation, however, is perhaps not so easy in those cases which do not presuppose any real salvation but in which the speaker takes up the position that something has already occurred and accordingly uses words which he would have employed if it had in fact been realized; then the Psalmist can exclaim that the wicked are gathered together against the righteous and oppress the innocent

> 'but Yahweh was (*wayᵉhî*) my high tower . . .
> 'and did bring back (*wayyāšeḇ*) upon them their (own) iniquity,'[1]

and the prophet can announce

> 'be glad then, ye children of Zion, and rejoice in the Lord your God; for He gave you the former rain in just measure
> 'and did make to come down (*wayyôreḏ*) the rain for you,'[2]

where the reason for rejoicing is clearly a past event regarded as an augury for future blessings.

The so-called 'prophetic perfect' is susceptible of similar explanation; it is not a prophetic peculiarity but is borrowed from the style of the hymns by prophets who were also poets, as in

> 'the earth has been polluted under her inhabitants, because they have transgressed the laws . . .
> 'therefore a curse has devoured the earth and there were found guilty (*wayye'šᵉmû*)[3] the inhabitants thereof.'[4]

It may also be remarked that the construction apparently occurs only in assertions uttered in prophetic hymns and never in purely prophetic announcements of disaster. Further, the prophets employ much historical matter which is not prophecy but illustrates what they have in mind; so in

> 'yet He also is wise and did bring (*wayyāḇē'*) evil, and he called not back his word,
> 'but he will arise against the house of evil-doers'[5]

[1] Ps. *94*. 22–23; cp. *16*. 9, *52*. 9 (s. p. 141).
[2] Jo. *2*. 23; cp. Is. *48*. 21, *59*. 15–17, Hab. *3*. 19.
[3] Or rather 'were appalled,' as *'āšēm* is here only a byform of *šāmēm*, as the Targûm takes it (cp. Hos. *5*. 15, *10*. 2, *14*. 1, Ps. *5*. 11, *34*. 22).
[4] Is. *24*. 5–6; cp. *ib*. 18.
[5] Is. *31*. 2; cp. Gen. *49*. 15. 24, Is. *9*. 7–21, Ezek. *23*. 16, *28*. 16, *31*. 12 (s. Birkeland in *Act. Orient.* XIII. 28).

both 'and did bring' and 'called not back' allude to the actual fact, of which men have had experience, that Yahweh has on occasion sent disaster as a means of chastisement, while only with 'but he will arise' comes the announcement of the punishment of the sin with which the speaker is concerned.

There is another class of passages which are held to support a present consecutive construction, but such an explanation of them may be ascribed to the misunderstanding of a common idiom. These are those in which it is announced, 'and Yahweh said (*wayyō'mer*)'[1] or 'and Jeremiah spoke (*wayᵉdabbēr*)'[2] or 'and I said (*wā'ōmar*)'[3] or 'and I answered and said (*wā'aʿan wā'ōmar*)';[4] these past tenses ought not to be turned into present time, since they are used because there is being written down what has already been said in past time.[5]

The usage here discussed seems to appear also in gnomic passages. So Job, speaking of the grave in general terms as a place where men find rest in death, asks why light and life are given to the unhappy

'who long for death . . . . . .
'and did dig for it (*wayyaḥpᵉrūhû*) more than for hid treasure,'[6]

where the participle is general but the following preterite refers to a particular case known to the speaker of persons seeking it like a hid treasure. So again the poet describes how the brooks are frozen over and heaped up with snow in winter or dry up and vanish out of sight in summer, so that

'the caravans circle around,[7] they go up into the waste and perish.
'The caravans of Tema looked, the convoys of Sheba waited for them;
'they were ashamed because they had hoped;[8] they came unto them and were ashamed (*wayyeḥpārû*)';[9]

here a general truth expressed in gnomic form lapses into narrative style describing a real event which the speaker has possibly seen with his own eyes or which has been described to him by an eye-witness. So similes are often expressed as a concrete image, as in

'as a cloud was consumed and did vanish away (*wayyēlaḵ*),
'so he that goes down to Sheol shall come up no more,'[10]

[1] *E.g.* Is. *3.* 16. [2] Jer. *34,* 6. [3] Mic. *3.* 1.
[4] Jer. *11.* 5. [5] S. pp. 145–146. [6] Jb. *3.* 21; cp. Ps. *49.* 7.
[7] Namely, *yᵉlappᵉṯû 'ōrᵉḥōṯ* (for *yillāpᵉṯû 'orḥōṯ*); the meaning is that the caravans, having missed the brooks, circle round and round in the vain hope of refinding them.
[8] Namely, *ḇāṭāḥû* (for *ḇāṭāḥ*). [9] Jb. *6.* 15–20. [10] Jb. *7.* 9.

where the disappearance of the dead is compared to the disappearance of a cloud, which perhaps had vanished as the speaker spoke, and in

'a man that is born of a woman is of few days and full of trouble;
'he came forth like a flower and did wither (*wayyimmāl*), and he fled (*wayyiḇraḥ*), and he does not continue,'[1]

where the general easily passes into the particular and back again.[2]

A similar construction may appear in conditions where the preterite tense is common, as in

'pride came in, and there came in (*wayyāḇō'*) shame,'[3]

namely, on some one occasion pride was observed by the original speaker to be followed by shame, and it may therefore be inferred that this does or will normally happen, so that the saying may be paraphrased 'when pride cometh, then cometh shame' (as in the R.V.). The usage may even be extended to impossible conditions, as in

'granted, I cried and he did answer me (*wayyaʿănēnî*),'[4]

which depicts an event which ought to have happened and cannot in fact now happen as though it has happened, so that it may be paraphrased 'if I had cried, then would he have answered me.' The use, too, of the preterite tense in future conditions must be similarly explained, however difficult the idiom may appear to a modern reader; such a passage is

'but a man did die and became prostrate (*wayyeḥĕlāš*),'[5]

which may be paraphrased 'when a man has died/dies, then he will have become/will be prostrate,' so that even here the figure is bound to past time.

It may then be accepted that an element of past time can be detected in many, possibly in most, cases of a supposed present consecutive imperfect or, as it ought to be called, preterite tense.[6] As Birkeland[7] says, this was a typical early Hebrew phenomenon which gradually disappeared from the

[1] Jb. *14*. 1–2.
[2] Cp. Jb. *39*. 15.
[3] Prov. *11*. 2.
[4] Jb. *9*. 16; cp. Is. *48*. 18–19.
[5] Jb. *14*. 10; cp. Ezek. *33*. 4, 6; Jb. *10*. 22.
[6] Birkeland (in *Act. Orient.* XIII. 30) rightly utters a caution concerning passages where the vocalization is suspicious, as in 'why art thou cast down, O my soul, and wast disquieted (*wattehmî*) upon me?' (Ps. *42*. 6), where the true reading is, 'and why art thou disquieted (*ūmah-tehmî*) upon me,' as the parallel passages and several of the Versions (LXX., Symm., Pesh.) show.
[7] In *Act. Orient.* XIII. 31–33.

language.[1] For, apart from the strong *wāw*, on which its preterite character depended, it was indistinguishable in form with the imperfect tense, from which too it was in many places indistinguishable also in usage ; hence under Aramaic influence [2] this preterite came to be submerged by the imperfect tense or to be replaced by the weak *wāw* with the perfect tense. This, however, makes caution necessary in applying this new explanation of the imperfect or preterite tense to any given example ; for it must always be remembered that there is no hard-and-fast rule in a living language and that there must have been much confusion in the choice of the appropriate construction when there still existed side by side two so closely similar forms of which one was dying out of and the other was coming into common use. Probably few, if any, of the actual speakers would have been able to explain the difference between the two forms or would have known in many cases which construction he was using, at any rate when the accentuation failed to make it clear to him.[3]

It is, of course, well known that certain particles in the Semitic languages have the same effect as the strong *wāw* in Hebrew, Moabite and Aramaic, and these sometimes take the apocopated form and sometimes the full imperfect form of the verb ; originally, however, there can be little doubt that the apocopated or preterite is the correct form with them and that, when they are followed by the imperfect tense, it is due to erroneous assimilation of the one to the other form. The clearest example of the apocopated form occurs in the passage beginning

'then assembled (*'āz yaqhēl*) Solomon the elders of Israel,' [4]

where the reduction of the final vowel in the final syllable from *î* to *ē* is the nearest approach to *yáqtul* as distinct from *yaqtúl* possible under the rules of Hebrew grammar ; but the interesting point is that in the parallel passage the Massoretes have, *ex hypothesi* incorrectly, corrected the preterite *yaqhēl* into the impossible *yaqhêl*, representing an approximation to the imperfect *yaqhîl*. So, too, in such idioms as 'then sang (*'āz*

[1] Cp. Ps. *33*. 9, with *148*. 5, for the replacement of the earlier strong *wāw* with the preterite or imperfect by the later weak *wāw* with the perfect tense (s. p. 139).

[2] Birkeland (in *Act. Orient.* XIII. 32) rightly observes that the fact that the consecutive preterite construction is found in an early Aramaic inscription (s. pp. 120–121) is proof that it was an archaic construction which disappeared from Aramaic at an earlier date than from Hebrew ; thus the same influences were at work in both languages.

[3] So the Germ. *war* and the Germ. *wäre* are now represented by the Engl. *was* both in principal and subordinate clauses ; for the Engl. *were* is rapidly dying out even amongst educated people.

[4] 1 Ki. *8*. 1=2 Chron. *5*. 2 (s. pp. 120–121) ; cp. 1 Sam. *2*. 10, where the apocopated *yārēm* may be a preterite tense referring to a definite historic event.

yāšîr) Moses '[1] in Hebrew, and 'then said he (*'iḏ yaqûlu*) to the believers '[2] in Arabic the imperfect form may be a vivid usage, employed because at the moment of speaking the act is not yet complete, when 'then was Moses singing' and 'then was he saying' is the correct translation; but, as such an explanation fails to suit many of the instances, it is easier to suppose that in both languages the imperfect has improperly usurped the functions of the almost extinct preterite tense. For, just as in

'our camels have not yet gone off (*lammâ yazul*) with our saddles,'[3]

so in

'so I went forth (*fa'aḫruju*) calling out and put on (*fa'albasu*) my coat of mail'

the preterite tense is expected. This impression is only strengthened by a comparison of the Hebrew tense in

'for he spoke, and it was (*wayyᵉhî*);
'he commanded, and it stood firm (*wayyaʿămōḏ*)'[4]

and the Arabic tense in

'then he said to him, Be; so he was (*fayakûnu*),'[5]

where the imperfect is either used vividly and must be translated 'and he was coming into being' or 'and he is'[6] or else has displaced the true preterite tense through a historical error in the development of the language. An analogous though less drastic change may be seen by comparing the post-exilic Hebrew idiom in the parallel

'let them praise him; for he commanded and they were created (*wᵉnibrā'û*),[7]

where the perfect has displaced the imperfect tense.

These arguments can be extended to the simple imperfect or rather preterite tense without the strong *wāw* or any other warning particle, whether in the apocopated or "jussive" form or in that of the Western imperfect tense, namely whether it is still accented as the proto-Semitic *yáqtul* or has been assimilated to the Western *yaqtul* (Hebrew *yiqṭōl*).[8]

The examples of an externally recognizable preterite tense,

[1] Exod. *15*. 1. [2] Qur'ân, *Sûr. 3*. 120 (s. pp. 145–146).
[3] S. pp. 91, 95. [4] Ps. *33*. 9. [5] Qur'ân, *Sûr. 3*. 52.
[6] Cp. *ibid. 3*. 42. [7] Ps. *148*. 5.
[8] This usage is apparently common in the Ugaritian texts from Râs Šamrah, where however it still requires examination and elucidation (s. Montgomery & Harris, *Ras Shamra*, 25–26).

and in

'the deeps did cover them (*yᵉḵasᵉyūmû*),
'they went down (*yārᵉḏû*) into the depths like a stone,'[1]

where the historical allusions are obvious and the parallelism shows that both tenses refer to past time.[2]

It may here be added that it is not impossible that traces of this archaic preterite usage have survived also in the common speech, especially when an apparent imperfect is parallel with a perfect tense,[3] as for example in

'what said these men and whence did they come (*yāḇō'û*) unto thee?';[4]

for it is hardly possible to bring such a use of the imperfect tense under the heading of a courteous entreaty;[5] such an explanation is plausible in the case of a direct address in the second person but is highly improbable in that of a reference to an absent enemy in the third person. In fact, it may be asked whether the imperfect as politely used in questions relating to past time was not in fact the preterite tense, of which the origin has been forgotten and which has survived as a colloquialism.

It may be worth while to add that Biblical Aramaic apparently provides two instances of an archaic preterite tense in the passages

'at the same time mine understanding returned (*yᵉṯûḇ*) unto me and for the glory of my kingdom my majesty and brightness returned (*yᵉṯûḇ*) unto me, and my counsellors and my lords sought (*yᵉḇaʿôn*) unto me; and I was established (*hoṯqᵉnaṯ*) in my kingdom and excellent greatness was added (*hûsăpāṯ*) unto me'[6]

and

'then the king arose (*yᵉqûm*) very early in the morning and went (*'ăzal*) in haste to the den of lions';[7]

for the construction may either represent a vivid use of the imperfect tense or be due to a confusion of the imperfect with the preterite tense.[8]

If then the Hebrew *yiqṭōl*, though used almost only as an imperfect in prose, still survived as an archaic preterite tense

[1] Ex. *15*. 5.
[2] Cp. Jb. *3*. 3; *15*. 7 *alq.*
[3] S. pp. 145–146.
[4] 2 Ki. *20*. 14=Is. *39*. 3.
[5] S. R. Driver, *Tenses*, § 39 γ.
[6] Dan. *4*. 33.
[7] *Ibid*. *6*. 20.
[8] Bauer (in *B.A.S.S.* VIII. i. 45) plausibly suggests that the construction is a Hebraism, and that the Aram. *bēh-zimnâ* 'at the same time' and *bē'ḏayin* 'then' in the first and second passages respectively are imitations of the Hebr. *'āz* 'then' with the imperfect (preterite) tense.

without a special particle in poetry, it will not be surprising that it is occasionally found there with weak instead of strong *wāw*. For example, in

'thine anger was turned away (*yāšōḇ*) and thou didst comfort me (*ūṯenaḥămēnî*),' [1]

a shortened preterite *yáqtul* is joined by weak *wāw* to an ordinary imperfect (or improper preterite) *yaqtúl*,[2] while the reverse is the case in

'he added (*yôsîp̄*) rebellion unto his sin . . .
'and multiplied (*weyereḇ*) his words against God.' [3]

Yet such a usage is historically incorrect in view of the connection of the Hebr. *wayyiqṭōl* with the Acc. *-ma iqṭul* and, although there is a tendency to substitute *ū* for *-ma* in Accadian verbal clauses, it is difficult not to suspect this idiom in Hebrew texts,[4] especially as the Massoretic reading and vocalization may differ in parallel passages.[5]

The final argument in support of a preterite beside an imperfect tense may be found in certain proper names. Thus the patriarch Jacob was called *Yaʿăqōḇ* 'he grasped the heel' and afterwards *Yiśrā'-ēl* 'God contended' because 'in the womb he took the heel (*ʿāqaḇ*) of his brother and by his strength he contended (*śārāh*) with God' as the prophet says.[6] So Ishmael was called *Yišmāʿēl* 'God heard' 'because Yahweh has heard (*šāmaʿ*) thy affliction,'[7] and Joseph was called *Yôsēp̄* 'He added' because 'Yahweh added (*yōsēp̄*) to me another son.'[8] Here then is a clear case where the preterite vocalization is correct; for the usual rendering 'Yahweh add to me another son' makes nonsense, since the child is already born. Inversely, the patriarch Levi is called *Lēwî* 'joined' because 'now this time (*i.e.* yet once again) was my husband joined (*yillāweh*) unto me,'[9] where too the customary translation 'now this time will my husband be joined unto me' spoils the sense. In each of the first three examples the preterite is explained by a perfect, in the fourth the perfect is explained by a preterite (wrongly assimilated to an imperfect)[10]; in none is an imperfect

[1] Is. *12*. 1.
[2] Probably the Massoretes understood the clause as a wish, as the Targum suggests, but the context requires a past tense, as the LXX saw.
[3] Jb. *34*. 37.
[4] *E.g.* cp. Ps. *90*. 3 with Is. *12*. 1 and Hos. *8*. 10, 13 with Job *34*. 37 (s. S. R. Driver, *Tenses*, §§ 84, 174).
[5] *E.g.* 2 Sam. *22*. 12=Ps. *18*. 12 and 2 Sam. *22*. 38=Ps. *18*. 38.
[6] Hos. *12*. 4. I accept (in order to avoid confusion, if for no other reason) the usual explanation of the verb in this name (s. Albright, in *J.B.L.* XLVI. 154–168, where 'God heals' is suggested as its meaning).
[7] Gen. *16*. 11 (J).
[8] Gen. *30*. 24 (J).
[9] Gen. *29*. 34 (J).
[10] S. pp. 89–91.

does not seem to be used like *yō'mar* as a stereotyped form introducing an address, it is probably nothing more than an instance of the old preterite tense surviving here as occasionally elsewhere [1] in the language of daily life.[2]

[1] Cp. S. R. Driver, *Tenses*, § 27 γ (where other examples are cited).
[2] S. p. 142.

XVI

Desiderative Constructions

The most disputed use of the perfect in Hebrew is in apparently precative or optative clauses.[1] Most indeed of the passages usually cited in support of this idiom can be otherwise explained; some are probably due to textual corruption and some are equivocal, in others the perfect is virtually 'prophetic' or rather retains something of the force of the old permansive. Yet the verbal forms in Marduk's command to the new moon, when he said

'thou dost/shalt shine (*nabâta*) with horns to determine the six days,

. . . .

'at the full moon mayst thou be in opposition (*lû šutamḫurāt*) . . . and shine thou (*bini*) backward,'[2]

are exactly parallel to those in the Psalmist's

'Save me (*hôšîʿēnî*) from the mouth of the lion,
'and from the horns of the wild-ox thou dost/shalt answer me (*ʿănîṯānî*)';[3]

in both permansive-perfects with a present-future sense alternate with imperatives. Another passage belonging to the same class is

'tell ye it not in Gath, weep not at all;
'roll thyself (*hiṯpallāštî*)[4] in the dust at Beth-le-Aphrah:
'pass ye away, thou inhabitant of Shaphir, in shameful nakedness;[5]
'the inhabitant of Zaanan does/shall not come forth,
'the wailing of Beth-ezri shall take from you the stay thereof,'[6]

[1] Cp. S. R. Driver, *Tenses*, § 20, where all the suggested instances are tabulated.

[2] Langdon, *Creation*, 160–161, v. 16–20.

[3] Ps. *22.* 22.

[4] Not the first but the dialectical (Aramaizing) feminine second person (s. Bauer & Leander, *Hist. Gr. d. hebr. Spr.* I. § 42 k).

[5] Namely, *ʿeryaṯ bōšeṯ* for *ʿeryāh ḇōšeṯ*.

[6] Mic. *1.* 10–11, where the variations between the singular and plural second persons are due to thinking now of the individual inhabitants and now of the collective populations of the places addressed.

where again the imperatives determine the force of the permansive-perfect form.[1]

The examples then of this construction, where it can hardly be evaded except by alteration of the consonantal text, are few; if, however, it is once admitted that the 'prophetic' perfect is a survival of the old universal usage of the permansive *qatil*, just as the preterite construction without a determining particle is really the old preterite *yaqtul* still maintaining a precarious existence, there can be no real objection to admitting the possibility and perhaps the actual traces of a precative or optative perfect in Hebrew.[2] Nor is it unfair to consider the date of the composition in which this idiom may be found, since it is not impossible that, being of genuine Semitic growth, it may have died out in classical but taken root again in Exilic or post-Exilic Hebrew under direct Accadian influence. The objection, therefore, to postulating such a construction is perhaps no greater in the later than in the earlier period. It is, however, in either case an archaism or a pseudo-archaism practically restricted to poetry. The objection that this usage in Syriac and Arabic is almost confined to peculiar forms and a limited number of idioms is not a valid argument against its occurrence in Hebrew; it merely means that, while in the latter language its scope remained something like that which it enjoyed in Accadian, though on an immeasurably restricted scale, in the former languages it has come to be thought unsuitable and accordingly to be increasingly restricted in practice.

An analogous idiom, almost as rare in Accadian as in Hebrew, occurs also in prose, where it is used for the sake of vividness, being generally preceded by some asseverative particle or phrase.[3] So Gehazi exclaims

> 'as Yahweh liveth, surely I will run (*kî-'im raṣtî*) after him and take somewhat of him,'[4]

just as Aziri writes in one of the letters from Tall-al-ʿAmârna saying

> 'lo! I and Hatib will come (*nilligam*) now indeed quickly; O Hai, let your heart know that I will arrive (*gaštāku*),'[5]

where the two permansive-perfect forms are exactly parallel.

Another difficult case of the perfect tense occurs in the

[1] Cp. Is. *43*. 9 (s. pp. 117–118).

[2] It may be remarked that such a construction is recognized by the LXX, even to the extent of mistranslation, as when they render *yāsaptā* by προσθες (Is. *26*. 15).

[3] S. R. Driver, *Tenses*, 19–20.

[4] 2 Ki. *5*. 20.

[5] Knudtzon, *A.-T. 166*. 12–16 (where *gaštāku* stands for *kašdāku*).

passage where Joseph, having interpreted the dream of Pharaoh's cup-bearer to him, adds the request

> 'surely if thou shalt have remembered me (*kî 'im-zᵉḵartanî*) when it shall be well with thee, then shall thou be pleased to show (*wᵉʿāśîṯā-nâ*) kindness unto me,'[1]

where both *kî 'im* and the perfect tense have been found difficult. Without *kî* the conditional clause is simple enough;[2] but, as *kî* taken separately is out of place in the context, it has been suggested that, if *kî 'im* (taken together) is translated 'surely,' the perfect *zᵉḵartanî* may have a precative or imperative force. If this were so, the passage might mean 'mayst thou' or 'thou shalt (do thou) remember me when it shall be well with thee, and mayst thou be' or 'thou shalt' or 'do thou be pleased to show kindness unto me'; but neither rendering is satisfactory, the first on grounds of grammar, the second on the score of sense.[3] Moreover, the attachment of the precative *nâ* to the second verb shows that the wish is expressed by that verb, and this implies that the first verb is not optative but conditional. Attempts have therefore been made not to solve but to evade the difficulty by altering the text. Such a drastic remedy, however, is not necessary, as the occurrence of the same idiom in one of the letters from Tall-al-ʿAmârna shows. There one Labaya, addressing his overlord the king of Egypt, says

> 'surely if (*kie šumma*) the king shall have written (*šapar*) unto my wife, surely (*kie*) I will keep her (*akalluši*); surely if (*kie šumma*) the king shall have written (*šapar*) unto me: Plunge a dagger of bronze into thine heart and die, surely (*kie*) I shall not do (*ippušu*)[4] the written order of the king.'[5]

Here the Acc. *kie šumma* (=*kī* or *kē*) with the perfect *šapar* exactly corresponds with the Hebr. *kî 'im* with the perfect *zᵉḵartanî*, while the following imperfect tense in the former corresponds with the perfect tense with consecutive *wāw* in the latter case. In each the perfect has the force of a future-perfect tense in a condition of which the protasis is regarded as unlikely; thus thereby Labaya suggests that such an order from the king is inconceivable and that, if it comes, he will not obey it and Joseph drops a delicate hint that, if such a person as the cup-bearer does anything so inconceivable as to remember a Hebrew prisoner when he is restored to his office, he will then certainly also be good enough to befriend him.

[1] Gen. *40*. 14 (E). [2] Cp. S. R. Driver, *Tenses*, § 138, i. *a*, ii. *a*. [3] *Ibid.* 142².
[4] Literally '(know) that I shall not do' (s. p. 77). [5] Knudtzon, *A.-T.* *254*. 38–46.

Finally, attention may be drawn to a peculiar use of the Acc. *lū* and the Hebr. *lû* which is commonly employed with the precative or permansive forms in Accadian, just as it is used with the perfect tense or the jussive form in Hebrew. Occasionally too it takes the present in Accadian just as once it takes the imperfect tense in Hebrew; thus the Acc. *lû allak* 'surely I will go'[1] corresponds roughly with the Hebr. *lû Yišmāʿēl yiḥyeh lᵉp̄ānêḵā* 'surely Ishmael shall live before thee!'[2] Both constructions are rare, but the fact that both the Acc. *lā* and the Hebr. *lō'* may take these tenses in mild prohibitions prevents their being thought surprising; moreover, both particles are used exceptionally with precative or jussive forms, as in 'let not indeed the king my lord say (*lâ-mi iqbā*)'[3] and 'only see that thou bring not (*lō' ṯāšēḇ*) my son thither again.'[4] Further, the verb in the Babylonian example has the emphatic ending *-ā* which recalls the fact that the Hebrew verb takes the cohortative *-āh* once in this construction in 'not so let me tarry (*lō'* . . . *'ōḥîlāh*) with thee.'[5] Rarest of all constructions in both languages is the use of the affirmative precative particle with the imperative mood. Two Babylonian examples are 'pray, have conveyed here (*lû šūbila*) three thousand talents of gold'[6] and 'pray, enquire of him (*lū* . . . *šalšu*) much.[7]' Of these passages the second comes from Persia, while the first comes from Palestine; thus it justifies the unique Hebrew example in 'pray, hearken unto us (*lû*[8] *šᵉmāʿēnû*), my lord'[9] and 'but if thou—pray, hearken unto us (*lû šᵉmāʿēnû*) . . .,'[10] and it may be safely inferred that the consonantal text is right, though wrongly vocalized by the Massoretes.

[1] Knudtzon, *A.-T. 164*. 34; cp. King in *R.A.* IX. 97, v. 14 (s. Ungnad, *Mat. z. altakk. Spr.* 60).

[2] Gen. *17*. 18.

[3] Knudtzon, *A.-T. 129*, 52.

[4] Gen. *24*. 8. So translated the indicative mood expresses a despairing wish; the R.V.'s 'Oh that Ishmael might live before thee!' is hardly possible without a jussive form.

[5] 1 Sam. *18*. 14.

[6] Knudtzon, *A.-T. 4*. 49.

[7] King & Thompson, *Behistun*, 200, *45*. 97.

[8] For *lô*, as vocalized in the M.T.

[9] Gen. *23*. 4–5, 14–15 (cp. v. 11, where too *lō'* is an error for *lū'*=*lû*).

[10] *Ibid*. 13. The anacoluthon recalls idioms like the Gr. οἶσθ' οὖν ὃ δρᾶσον. (Aristophanes, *Knights*, 1158).

XVII

Conclusion

Hebrew tradition in the account of Abraham's coming from the Babylonian city of Ur through Haran into Palestine preserves the recollection, however dim and distant, of a Babylonian element,[1] the Deuteronomist makes definite mention of an Aramæan,[2] and Ezekiel speaks equally definitely of an Amorite as well as a Hittite, *i.e.* a non-Semitic, strain[3] in the Hebrew people; in other words, according to their own traditions the Hebrews must have been a mixed nation, drawn principally from the neighbouring Semitic races but containing also a certain amount of foreign blood. Moreover the *Ḫabiru*, who may be held, even if not to be the Biblical Hebrews, at any rate to have contributed an element to the Hebrew stock, must have been a mixed horde of robbers composed of refugees and outlaws from the surrounding nations, largely Semites, lying between the Elamite mountains and the Mediterranean sea. It will then be natural to find something of this heterogeneous origin reflected in the Hebrew language; for the speech of a people normally reflects its origin.

Clearly the two main strands of which Hebrew is woven are Accadian and Aramæan; of Amorite, the third strand, little can be said in the present absence of any real knowledge, but it must probably have been something between Aramæan and proto-Arabic, of which too hardly anything is known. Yet it must not be supposed that Hebrew is a pure and simple mixture of Accadian and Aramæan as known within historical times; there must have been a proto-Semitic element in it, a primitive and purely Hebrew nucleus will have been another component part of it, and the process of fusion must have begun well before and may have continued well into the historic period. Within this period the traces of fusion are clear. Thus the early legends of Genesis are not merely stories based on proto-Semitic mythology as handed down in Accadian literature but actually contain not a few verbal echoes of the Accadian versions, while there is a sprinkling of Accadian words which must have come into the language while yet in the making; for they are found even in the earliest remnants of Hebrew literature. Further, there survive in the Old Testament indisputable signs of a dialect in northern Palestine closely resembling the neighbouring

[1] Gen. *11*. 27–*12*. 9. [2] Deut. *26*. 5. [3] Ezek. *16*. 3, 45.

P. 39.—Speiser (in *J.A.O.S.* LVI. 33–46) explains the feminine -(*a*)*t* as originally an accusative ending akin to the *t* in the Hebr. *'ēṯ* and so on introducing the direct object and the infixed *t* in the *ta-* themes of the verb; if this is so, it must have been originally a deictic or demonstrative element like the Eg. *t-* used as a definite article and so analogous to the accusative *-a* which is of the same nature, since its function too is at bottom directional (s. pp. 78–79).

P. 66.—If the Hebr. *ḥāraṣ* is not transitive but intransitive in meaning, the proper translation of *lō' ḥāraṣ 'îš* (for M.T.'s *l*[e]*'îš*) . . . *'eṯ-l*[e]*šōnô* (Josh. *10.* 21) is not 'none whetted his tongue . . .' (R.V.) but 'none was sharp of tongue . . .' (cp. Gen. *17.* 11, 14 and 1 K. *15.* 23 for this use of the accusative sign).

P. 79.—This energic *-n* (s. p. 40) appears also in early Aramaic texts (*e.g.* Cowley, *Aram. Pap. 8.* 10, *'Aḥ.* 82, 119).

P. 92.—Yet it may be remarked that Greek transliterations of Hebrew words seem hardly to recognize the strong *wāw*: all but two out of fifteen cases of it which appear in transliteration are apparently shown as weak *wāw* (s. Hatch & Redpath, *Concordance to the Septuagint*, II. 1026–1039, *Suppl.*, 211); but this phenomenon may be due to misinterpretation.

P. 102.—Rubens (in *J.Q.R.* X. 544) takes the Hebr. *'āz* as another relative pronoun parallel with the Phœn. *'z* in place of the normal Hebr. *zeh* once in the Old Testament (Ps. *69.* 5).

Pp. 132–133.—Yet in 'and Jacob rent his garments and put sack-cloth upon his loins and mourned (*wayyiṯ'abbēl*) for his son many days' (Gen. *37.* 34; cp. Neh. *1.* 4) the preterite tense describes not a momentary act but an activity continued over a number of days; such a usage is mostly easily explained as an extension of that whereby the same tense is applied to an act repeated a definite number of times (s. p. 121).

P. 141.—A gnomic use of the preterite tense may be seen in the Psalmist's 'like the deaf adder (which) stoppeth (*yaṭ'ēm*) its ear(s)' (Ps. *58.* 5), since the verb is not a Qal form with *ē* in the imperfect but an apocopated imperfect or rather a true preterite tense from the Hip̄'îl (s. pp. 69–71).

Pp. 151–152.—Apart from the well-known Aramaisms in the North-Palestinian sections of 'Judges' and 'Kings,' it is interesting to observe how many can be detected also in the work of the Ephraimite Hosea (s. G. R. Driver in *J.T.S.* XXXVI. 294–296).

SELECT BIBLIOGRAPHY OF PERIODICAL LITERATURE

1877

A. H. Sayce . . . 'The Tenses of the Assyrian Verb' (in *J.R.A.S.*, N.S. IX. 22–58).

1878

P. Haupt . . . 'Studies on the Comparative Grammar of the Semitic Languages' (in *J.R.A.S.*, N.S. X. 244–251).

1885

J. F. M'Curdy . . 'The Semitic Perfect in Assyrian' (in *Actes du VI*^{me} *Congrès International des Orientalistes*, II. i. 507–534).

1887

J. Barth . . . *Das semitische Perfekt im Assyrischen* (in *Z.A.* II. 375–386).

G. Hoffmann . . *Nöldeke, T. H.: Die semitischen Sprachen. Eine Skizze* (in *Lit. Centralbl.* 1887, 605–608).

J. Wellhausen . . *Th. Nöldeke, Die semitischen Sprachen. Eine Skizze* (in *D. Lz.* VIII. 966–968).

1889

J. Barth . . . . *Vergleichende Studien* III. *Das i-Imperfect im Nord-semitischen* (in *Z.D.M.G.* XLIII. 177–191).

1890

F. Hommel . . . *Uebersicht über die . . . Bildung des Nomina. Von Paul de Lagarde* (in *Z.D.M.G.* XLIV. 535–548).

M. Lambert . . . *Observations sur la théorie des formes nominales de M. Barth* (in *J.A.* VIII. xv. 164–179).

H. Zimmern . . . *Das Verhältniss des assyrischen Permansivs zum semitischen Perfect und zum ägyptischen „Pseudoparticip" untersucht unter Benutzung der El-Amarna Texte* (in *Z.A.* V. 1–22).

1891

J. A. Knudtzon . . *Zur assyrischen und allgemein semitischen Grammatik* (in *Z.A.* VI. 405–431).

1892

J. A. Knudtzon . . *Zur assyrischen und allgemein semitischen Grammatik* (in *Z.A.* VII. 33–63).

1893

R. Brünnow . . . *Beiträge zur assyrischen und vergleichenden semitischen Sprachwissenschaft, herausgegeben von Friedrich Delitzsch und Paul Haupt. Zweiter Band, Heft 2 . . . 1892* (in *Z.A.* VIII. 125–142).

J. A. Knudtzon . . *Vom sogenannten Perfekt und Imperfekt im Hebräischen* (in *Actes du 8*^{me} *Congrès International des Orientalistes*, I. ii. 71–83).

M. Lambert . . . *Le vav conversif* (in *R.É.J.* XXVI. 47–62).

INDEX

1. SUBJECT-MATTER

2. SCHOLARS

3. BIBLICAL PASSAGES

GENESIS.

PRINTED BY MORRISON AND GIBB LTD., EDINBURGH AND LONDON

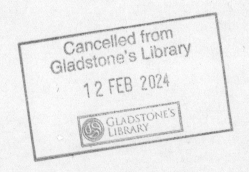